ALLEN BREED SERIES

The Allen Breed Series examines horse and pony breeds from all over the world, using a broad interpretation of what a breed is: whether created by the environment where it originally developed, or by man for a particular purpose: selected for its useful characteristics, or for its appearance, such as colour. It includes all members of the horse family, and breeds with closed or protected stud books as well as breeds and types still developing.

Each book in the Allen Breed Series examines the history and development of the breed, its characteristics and use, and its current position in Britain, together with an overview of the breed in America and worldwide. More difficult issues are also tackled, such as particular problems associated with the breed, and such controversies as the effect of the show ring on working breeds. The breed societies and their role in modern breeding policies are discussed.

BOOKS IN THE SERIES

The Appaloosa
The Fell Pony
The Hanoverian
The Irish Draught
The Mule
The Trakehner

ALLEN BREED SERIES

The Trakehner

Frontispiece: Statue of Tempelhüter in front of the *Landstallmeister* house at the Trakehnen central stud's main farm.

ALLEN BREED SERIES

The Trakehner

Eberhard von Velsen and Erhard Schulte

Translated by
Christina Belton

with additional material by
Celia Clarke

J. A. Allen
London

British Library Cataloguing in Publication Data
Velsen, Eberhard von
    The Trakehner.
    1. Trakehner horses
    I. Title   II. Schulte, Erhard   III. Trakehner. *English*
    636.13

    ISBN 0–85131–479–1

First published in Germany in 1981 by Franckh'sche
Verlagshandlung, W. Keller & Co., Stuttgart

Published in Great Britain in 1990 by
J. A. Allen & Company Limited
1 Lower Grosvenor Place, London SW1W 0EL
English translation and additional material,
© J. A. Allen & Company Limited 1990

Editor Elizabeth O'Beirne-Ranelagh
Book production Bill Ireson
Printed and bound in Great Britain by
St Edmundsbury Press Limited, Bury St Edmunds, Suffolk

Contents

Cover design by Siegfried Fischer (photo: Werner Ernst), showing three mares from the Zauberspiel (by Impuls) line at the Argenhof stud (Baden-Württemberg).

Endpapers: Two-year-old colts at the Trakehnen stud's Neu-Budupönen farm in the 1930s.

Preface

There is surely no breed of horse existing today whose history and geography mirrors the changing fortunes of Northern Europe since the Middle Ages as closely as the 'Warmblood Horse of Trakehner Origin', or Trakehner, as it is better known.

From its Schweiken ancestors, the preferred cavalry horse of the Teutonic knights, to its present name, which comes from the Trakehnen Stud where selected members of the breed were used to produce a high-class, all-round horse exclusively for the use of the royal household of Friedrich Wilhelm II of Prussia, its background is resonant with history. Indeed, the very fact that it is now known as the Trakehner breed, rather than as the East Prussian (which it was often called before the end of the Second World War), signifies that the numerical strength of the breed, and its original homeland in East Prussia, were both major casualties of the Russian advance westwards in the final years of the war.

The 'flight of the East Prussian horses' from their homelands in the most easterly parts of Prussia, through what became Poland and East Germany, to safety in what became West Germany is one of the great sagas of equine and human history. Much of the flight took place in the bitterly cold months of December 1944 and January and February 1945, with many of the mares in foal and practically every adult horse harnessed to the now famous 'trek waggons', in which were carried any possessions the fleeing owners were able to rescue. The loss of stock left behind in Russian-occupied territory and in Poland, and the harsh conditions encountered on the flight, meant that only about 1600 horses out of an original stud book numbering nearly 27,000 survived to settle in West Germany in 1945. In addition, the refugee status of their owners, plus the very difficult economic conditions in West Germany during the following two years, decreased the breed still further in numbers, until only about 700 mares and 60 stallions survived.

In 1947, in a determined bid to save the breed from extinction, Siegfried Freiherr von Schrocten and Dr Fritz Schilke (respectively chairman and secretary of the original East Prussian stud book society, the *Ostpreussische Stutbuchgesellschaft*) collected and identified the horses, founded the Trakehner *Verband* to take over the organisation of the records and created a regional breeding structure for Trakehner breeding in West Germany, with studs and stallions in each breeding area. From being a homeless breed, the Trakehner at once became the only national West German breed, with a structure that would influence all aspects of warmblood

1

breeding throughout the country. Because warmblood breeding in Germany was originally designed to produce both horses for all kinds of military work, and light draught horses for use in agriculture, with the production of competition horses only becoming a major factor in the postwar years, almost from the beginning the vast majority of breeders were local farmers who used stallions supplied by the local breeding societies or large landowners, and this structure, which still applies today, benefited considerably from a sizeable influx of Trakehner blood.

It is important, when studying warmblood breeding, to bear in mind that before German unification in 1871, Germany was made up of a number of different states, and the locally organised breeding areas under the control of a local breed society reflected this structure. As a result, horses bred in the Hanover area therefore became known as Hanoverians, those bred in the Schleswig-Holstein area became known as Holsteins, those bred in Westphalia became known as Westphalians and so on, with this structure still being maintained today by the controlling national organisation, the *Deutschen Landwirtschafts-Gesesllschaft* or DLG (the German Ministry of Agriculture). However, although the Trakehner *Verband* is under the overall control of the DLG, members of the Trakehner breed are an honourable exception to this breed-naming rule, as they are still known as Trakehners wherever they are foaled.

However, although the generally accepted definition of a warmblood – a European performance horse developed by upgrading native mares through the controlled use of infusions of selected and performance-tested outside blood – applies to the Trakehner, over the last two centuries it has developed into a type of breed distinct from those originating from the other German breeding areas, such as Oldenburg, Hanover and Westphalia, which have become very similar to each other and are often impossible to recognise individually without examining the horse's brand. This is because the Trakehner is the only 'pure' breed of warmblood type. Unlike the other regional breed societies, who have used many of the same sires, regardless of breed (with popular stallions being graded into two, three or even four different stud books), the Trakehner breeding authorities in West Germany only allow up-grading through the limited use of high-quality Thoroughbred, Anglo-Arab and Arab stallions, who are graded into the breeding stud books alongside stallions with Trakehner blood. Once graded into the breeding stud book these stallions add XX to their names if they are Thoroughbreds (e.g. Perfectionist XX), X to their names if they are Anglo-Arabs (e.g. Inspector X) and OX to their names if they are Arabs (e.g. Fetysz OX) to denote their origin in the pedigrees of their progeny. Their progeny out of graded Trakehner mares are then treated as 'purebred' despite their mixed origins, with the word 'partbred' being used to describe crosses between a graded Trakehner and an animal not graded into the Trakehner stud book.

As has always been the tradition within the Trakehner breed, horses bred today are still given names starting with the first letter of their dam's names, unlike the practice in many other warmblood breeds where foals have to begin their names with the initial letter of the sire's name. This reflects the importance given to the mare families, whose influence still permeates the breed today, and who are numbered for easy identification (e.g. the famous mares Kassette and Kokette belonged to family no. 57, which traces from a black mare Kleebat born in 1780 by Brutus I, while the double DLG champion Polarfahrt belonged to family no. 137).

In recent years the modern Trakehner has become a more elegant animal than was the case in immediate prewar days, and it is highly prized both as a competition horse in itself, and as a source of 'upgrading' blood for the heavier warmblood breeds. Its strong stud book reflects this success, with over 1400 foals being born each year and over 4000 registered Trakehners living in West Germany alone, while its influence on the younger warmblood breeds (such as the Dutch Warmblood, the Danish Warmblood and the British Warmblood) is considerable, as is its popularity with North American breeders and riders. Following its amazing recovery from the low point of 1945, the future for the Trakehner breed looks assured for many years to come.

1 The beginnings of horse breeding in East Prussia

In no other region of Germany did the horse play such an important role as in East Prussia (see p. 28). The region had all the necessary characteristics for breeding horses: it had the right climate, good fields and an agricultural economy. Furthermore, its people had a natural enthusiasm for breeding and riding fine horses.

The first attempts at organised horse breeding in this area date back to the times of the Teutonic Order around A D 1500. The knights belonging to this order wanted to breed from the indigenous horses, known as the 'Schweiken', which were small and very hardy. It was decided to breed the Schweiken in estate studs, separately from the heavy horses. (The heavy horses, used in hand-to-hand combat, were brought from their native countries by the knights.) The Schweiken were blue-dun in colour, with an eel stripe along their backs and zebra marks on their legs. Primitive colouring and markings showed them to be direct descendants of the ancient 'Tarpan' breed. The aim of the breeding programme was to increase the size and weight of the horses and therefore produce a more versatile type of animal. The Schweiken was developed into a useful general purpose work horse, whilst the heavy horses continued to be used for riding and combat. These general purpose horses went on to form the basis for the development of the light cavalry.

It is known from contemporary documents that at the beginning of the sixteenth century there were about sixty private studs on estates in East Prussia. They were mostly around Marienburg, Danzig, Elbing, Tapiau and Ragnit. But the decline of chivalry meant that horse breeding fell into a state of neglect. Breeding of the heavy combat horses almost disappeared. It continued, on a very small scale, only in Ermland.

However, organised breeding of the Schweiken was practised once again on a fairly large scale in the seventeenth century, but horse breeding fell into decline once more at the beginning of the eighteenth century because of outbreaks of the plague, which killed large numbers of people in East Prussia. The revival of the region's economy was due to the foresight and planning of Friedrich Wilhelm I (1713–1740). On the suggestion of Prince Leopold of Anhalt-Dessau, the Prussian king undertook the cultivation of marshy areas. The Gumbinnen, Stallupönen, Ebenrode and Insterburg regions in particular (later to become the main breeding zone of the

4

'Warmblood Horse of Trakehner Origin') contained large areas of marshland. This was the region where the plague had hit particularly hard, with widespread loss of life. From all over Europe new settlers came to the area, including Huguenots from France and Holland and Protestants from the Salzburg region. They drained and cleared the land and made it suitable for agriculture.

In 1726 Friedrich Wilhelm I decided to bring together the horses from studs at Guddin, Ragnit, Grunhof, Insterburg, Königsberg and others to form one central stud. This was necessitated by the greatly increased demand for cavalry remounts and horses for the royal stables. The king felt that he himself must assume responsibility for breeding and supplying horses for military purposes.

The area chosen by Friedrich Wilhelm I was about 3500 hectares (8600 acres) in size and lay north of Rominter Heath, between Gumbinnen and Stallupönen near the estate known as 'Trakehnen'. The name of the estate dated from the beginning of the sixteenth century and came from the Lithuanian word 'Trakis' used to describe the place, meaning 'burnt land'. This description was a reference to the cultivation, clearance and 'burning off' of the land which had taken place around that time. Although it was not until the eighteenth century that Trakehnen became a large state-owned stud, exercising a considerable influence on horse breeding, it should be noted that by this time the local people in this area had already been breeding utility horses successfully for 200 years.

By the beginning of the seventeenth century there were already a number of large, private studs with their own carefully kept stud books, some of which are still in existence. Particularly notable is the Dohna-Schlobitten stud, which in 1623 already had six stallions and twenty-four mares on its books, and which is referred to by writers of the time as the oldest of these studs. Studs were also owned by Counts Finckenstein, Kalnein, Schwerin and Eulenburg, and the von Buddenbrook, von Saucken, von Bieberstein and von der Gröben families. There were also some large studs belonging to ecclesiastical princes, for example the episcopal studs of Marienwerder, Georgenburg, Schmoleinen and Bischdorf.

The establishment of private studs, the breeding of utility horses by farmers, and the formation of the central Trakehnen stud and the regional studs meant that by the middle of the eighteenth century, under the control of the state, the basis had been established for the now world-famous 'East Prussian Warmblood of Trakehner Origin'.

2 The foundations of organised breeding

The Trakehnen Central Stud

The founding of the stud and the early days

The official beginning of organised horse breeding in East Prussia is 1732, the year the Trakehnen Central Stud was founded. On the orders of Friedrich Wilhelm I, father of Frederick the Great, 1100 horses were brought to the 'Royal Trakehnen Stud'. Among these were about 500 broodmares. The horses came from various state-owned properties, the so-called 'royal horse breeding departments' which were to be found all over East Prussia. The first horses based at Trakehnen represented various European breeds. The main breeds were Neapolitan, Danish, Andalusian, and Oriental, as well as riding horses imported from England. The main stallions used in the eighteenth century were of Oriental descent. This created an imbalance in the broodmare stock which, at first, prevented the stud making much progress in its breeding programme. In 1739 the crown prince (the future Frederick the Great) received the unprofitable Trakehnen stud as a present. Chancellor von Domhardt, who was the governor of Gumbinnen, took over as director of the stud, which, by royal decree, was only to supply horses – mainly carriage horses and parade horses – for the royal stables. During this period there seems to have been no particular breeding policy.

In the period from 1732 to 1782 a total of 356 stallions were used at Trakehnen. However, only a few of these stallions, namely some Oriental horses and some quality English horses, achieved good results and left their stamp on the broodmare stock. Particularly worthy of note are the English stallion Pitt, who was descended from the Darley Arabian, his grandson Adler, the Persian stallion Spinola and other Oriental stallions such as Bassa, Hannibal and, in particular, the grey Persianer. The oldest mare lines in the Trakehner stud book today can be traced back to these stallions.

In 1779, against Frederick the Great's wishes, von Domhardt allocated eleven stallions for the use of the private breeders of East Prussia, a beneficial move with far-reaching implications. This he did after being refused permission to set up a separate stallion station. His action met with so much approval from the local breeders and was so successful, that the king finally allowed von Domhardt to increase the number of stallions to twenty.

Today it is clear that his action marked the beginning of the improvement of the East Prussian horse, and so of the German horse, through a system of regional studs and a central stud. This system has been in operation for over 200 years.

At the end of the eighteenth century a number of private studs, still famous today, became established names, including those of von Simpson (Georgenburg), von Zitzewitz (Weedern), von Sperber (Lenken), von Kuenheim (Juditten), and Count Rautter (Willkamm).

After the death of Frederick the Great in 1786, Trakehnen passed into the hands of the state. It was at this point that an organised breeding programme was drawn up and implemented. For the first time broodmares were selected on the basis of their breeding and correct conformation. Any animal which did not satisfy the requirements was withdrawn and put up for sale.

Friedrich Wilhelm II, the successor of Frederick the Great, did much to promote East Prussian horse breeding. Knowledgeable as well as enthusiastic, he appointed Count Karl Lindenau (1786–1814), who enjoyed the reputation of being the major authority on horses at the time, as stud manager at Trakehnen. His first action was to set up more stallion stations: these were to become the regional state studs of Insterburg, Oletzko, Ragnit and Marienwerder. Trakehnen itself remained the central stud and the regional stud for its area. A total of 269 stallions were bought and distributed among the regional centres. At the same time, on the advice of Count Lindenau, the mares were subjected to rigorous selection procedures. Only quality mares were allowed to be covered by state stallions. The inferior ones were not allowed to be used for breeding.

In 1787, Count Lindenau carried out a general inspection of the entire horse stock at Trakehnen. Twenty-five of the thirty-eight stallions in use and 144 of the 356 mares were rejected! Following this beneficial move, all foals born at the central stud were branded on the right thigh with the single seven-pronged elk antler (see p. 107).

In 1786, Count Lindenau appointed Herr von Brauchitsch as the first *Landstallmeister*, with his headquarters in the great house at Trakehnen. The broodmares belonging to the central stud were kept at five different farms, with mares of riding type going to Alt-Trakehnen and Bajohrgallen, and those of the carriage-horse type going to Kalpakin, Gurdzen and Guddin. The herds were also divided up according to colour, i.e. black, bay, chestnut, and two mixed herds. Colour segregation remained in operation right up until the flight from Trakehnen in 1945.

Trakehnen under Landstallmeisters von Burgsdorff and von Schwichow

During the Revolutionary and Napoleonic wars the central stud suffered heavy losses, as did the whole of the East Prussian horse breeding industry. Valuable breeding stock, both mares and stallions, were among the horses requisitioned by the enemy. In this period of decline Friedrich Wilhelm III appointed the former director of the West Prussian stud, Friedrich-Wilhelm von Burgsdorff, as *Landstallmeister* of Trakehnen. He was a pupil of Count Lindenau, and knew Trakehnen and its horses

Thunderclap by Mickle Fell XX, a stallion at the central Trakehnen stud who greatly influenced the chestnut herd in the early nineteenth century. His Anglo-Arab pedigree is borne out by his appearance, and his bloodline survived at Trakehnen into modern times.

well. As his main task he set about buying outstanding stallions from England and the East. In a relatively short time he restored Trakehnen to its former glory. He brought to Trakehnen the famous Turk Main Atty and twelve of his sons from a stud at Neustadt in Brandenburg. These stallions had considerable influence on Trakehner breeding. Von Burgsdorff was also responsible for breeding the famous Thunderclap, who stamped the stock at Trakehnen with his own particular mark for decades. From England he brought the purebred Arabian, Nedjed OX, who produced some superlative breeding stock. It was under von Burgsdorff that the first Thoroughbred mares arrived at Trakehnen. These were to found female lines which have remained some of the most valuable in Trakehner breeding, among them the Handschelle, Herbstzeit and Halensee lines.

In the period 1815–1819 the number of farms attached to the stud was increased to nine with the purchase of Danzkehmen and Taukenischken. The breeding stock consisted of 300 broodmares and sixteen stallions, and the total horse population at Trakehnen was about 1000, which placed it numerically ahead of the studs at Graditz and Neustadt. In fact it was by far the largest state stud in the western world at the time.

The Trakehner horses already enjoyed a very good reputation, since they made coach horses of exceptional stamina, and very tough cavalry horses. It was also *Landstallmeister* von Burgsdorff who was responsible for introducing the principle of pure-breeding: during his period of office no outside blood was introduced except English Thoroughbred and purebred Arabian. The use of these two breeds in Trakehner breeding did not count as outcrossing, as is still the case in most warmblood breeding today, although other warmblood breeds do accept animals of other origins as well, which Trakehner breeders do not.

Von Burgsdorff's successor, Alexander von Schwichow (1847–1864), was equally talented and knowledgeable in the field of horse breeding. He was responsible for consolidating the broodmare herds. At the same time he established the East Prussian horse as a set 'type' which has remained unchanged. He was also responsible for introducing into the breeding programme some important stallions which left their mark on the breed, for example Thunderclap, who has already been mentioned, Sahama XX, Inspector X, Snyders XX, Collino, and the half brothers Venerato and Vorwärts. Trakehnen's main task at this time was to supply stallions for the regional studs, and so to determine the direction of East Prussian warmblood breeding. It was also responsible for supplying remounts every year for the royal stables and the army. One notable reason for von Schwichow's success was his policy of intensive grassland management. He also introduced richer feeding, realising that, for their development, quality horses needed the best possible management.

Breeding for more substance: the stud under Landstallmeister von Dassel

Von Schwichow's successor, Gustav Adolph von Dassel, tried to give the Trakehner more substance by introducing three Anglo-Norman stallions and the Hanoverian stallion Solon. This attempt to introduce 'outside' blood met with opposition from the breeders. The latter, who constituted a large group, were firmly convinced that the policy of keeping the breed pure should continue; East Prussian horses had been very successful as cavalry horses and farmhorses, and at exhibitions. This point of view was reinforced by events such as a German farmers' exhibition held in 1863, where the privately bred East Prussian horses were described afterwards as being the 'stars of the show' on account of their uniformity and their quality. Not only the horses from the big studs but also those produced by the small farmers are described in authenticated reports as being of high quality.

Landstallmeister von Dassel obtained good results with Thoroughbred stallions such as Friponnier XX, Hector XX, Duke of Edinborough XX and Marsworth XX. They reinforced the reputation of the central stud as the cornerstone of the entire Prussian horse-breeding industry. Thoroughbred/Trakehner crosses from the central stud, such as Flügel, Malteser, Tunnel, Thebaner, Eberhard, Fürstenberg, Venezuela, Passvan and Orcus, were also equally important.

Landstallmeister von Franckenberg und Proschlitz (1888–1895) was responsible for breeding the famous Morgenstrahl, to whom a memorial was later erected in front of Trakehnen castle. This important bay stallion founded the Parsival–Hirtensang line which enjoys such renown today.

Increased Thoroughbred influence under Landstallmeisters von Oettingen and the Count von Sponeck

From 1895 to 1912 the famous *Landstallmeister* Burchard von Oettingen, formerly director of the state stud at Gudwallen and the Beberbeck central stud, was in office. 'Iis first act was to bring in the Beberbeck stallions Obelisk, Optimus and Lehnsherr, the effect of which was to give the breed more substance. However, his next move, at the beginning of the twentieth century, was to start upgrading the Trakehner by

The most important Thoroughbred at Trakehnen was Perfectionist XX, a grandson of St Simon. In only three seasons (from 1904 to 1907) he produced numerous stallions, among them the central stud's Jagdheld, Tempelhüter and Irrlehrer, together with many highly talented competition horses and mares with reliable breeding points.

increased use of English Thoroughbred blood. It was he who was responsible for buying the legendary Thoroughbred Perfectionist XX in England in 1903. The sum of 20,000 Gold Marks was paid, which was a high price for the time. In only three seasons, this horse produced breeding stock of uniformly high quality. Among his numerous offspring were Tempelhüter, Jagdheld and Irrlehrer, the founders of famous sire lines.

The fact that the Thoroughbred exercised an enormous influence on Trakehner breeding can be proven by statistics: 300 mares were covered by the twelve Thoroughbred stallions at Trakehnen, while the seven Thoroughbred/Trakehner crosses were allocated a total of only 100 mares. The reason for this can be found in the fact that at the time the province of East Prussia was supplying about 7000 remounts per year to the cavalry. Consequently the horse-breeding industry was in a sense dependent on the demands of the army, which required fast, manoeuvrable performance horses with a high proportion of Thoroughbred blood.

However, these horses did not meet the requirements of the agricultural sector and had insufficient pulling power. This resulted in the large landowners having to use coldbloods or draught horses for farm work. The small peasant farmers, however, used their highly bred East Prussian mares about the farm.

The horses at the central stud were kept in herds, watched over by mounted herdsmen. *Landstallmeister* von Oettingen was responsible for fencing the vast areas of meadowland at Trakehnen into enclosures. He was also the breeder of the influential stallions Prinz Optimus, Polarsturm, Jenissei, Fischerknabe and Elfenbein, and created the famous Trakehnen hunts, in which the three- and four-year-old horses from the 'hunting stable' took part. 'Performance testing' of this type placed high demands on the stamina and constitution of the young Trakehners and on their ability to gallop. Having undergone this rigorous testing, they were then offered for sale at the famed Trakehner auctions, which attracted buyers from all parts of the German Reich and from abroad.

Many of the young broodmares were also tested in the hunting field. Some of them performed exceptionally; for example, the daughter of Nana Sahib X, Panna, as well as being a successful broodmare, was also the best hunter at Trakehnen. She is the foundation mare of the Peraea and Pelargonie lines which are now very influential in West Germany. Another daughter of Nana Sahib, the mare Cymbal, had a great capacity for performance and great toughness. She later became the dam of the famous stallion Cancara.

In 1912, von Oettingen's son-in-law, the Count von Sponeck, succeeded him as *Landstallmeister*. He had previously been director of the studs at Braunsberg and Gudwallen. Von Oettingen succeeded Georg, Count von Lehndorff (1880–1912), as *Oberlandstallmeister*. Von Lehndorff had enjoyed the reputation of being the foremost authority on horses of his time. Trakehnen and the entire Prussian stud administration was under the control of the *Oberlandstallmeister*. While holding this post, von Oettingen founded, in 1926, the stallion testing station at Zwion bei Georgenburg. Three-year-old stallions destined for service as sires in the provincial studs were sent to this centre for a year's training. The training period ended with a test in which the horse's nature, temperament, basic paces, 'rideability', soundness, food utilisation and performance capabilities were evaluated, along with the marks it had received during its training. Only those stallions which passed the rigorous testing were entitled to take their places as stallions at the provincial studs. Unsuccessful stallions were not used for breeding.

Count von Sponeck, himself a successful jockey, increased the amount of Thoroughbred blood yet again during his term of office as *Landstallmeister*, raising the number of Thoroughbred stallions at the central stud to fourteen. There were nineteen stallions standing at the stud in all. However, the three most important stallions of this period, which lasted until 1922, were Tempelhüter, Nana Sahib X and Cancara. They produced the performance horses which rose to fame in the equestrian sport of the time. An important part was also played by the stallions Jagdheld, Master Magpie XX, Christian de Wet XX and Polarfischer, plus a large

Tempelhüter, foaled in 1905, was considered the ideal Trakehner and was also extremely successful as a sire, standing at stud from 1909 to 1932. His female progeny were the most valuable mares in the Trakehnen herd.

13

One of the great names in the history of Trakehner breeding was Cancara by Master Magpie XX out of Cymbal by Nana Sahib X. Foaled in 1917, this remarkable horse was an untiring performer in the sporting field, and also transmitted his qualities to his progeny. His daughters Donna and Kokette were two of the most outstanding broodmares in the history of West German Trakehner breeding.

number of Thoroughbred stallions whose descendants spread Trakehnen's fame around the world. Those among them who achieved the highest levels of success in sport are discussed in Chapter 4.

Breeding for more substance, and the period of consolidation: the stud under Landstallmeisters von Lehndorff and Ehlert

Von Sponeck's successor was the former director of Graditz: Siegfried, Count von Lehndorff. A son of *Oberlandstallmeister* Georg, Count von Lehndorff, discussed above, he had all the right qualifications for running a stud of Trakehnen's calibre. It is he who deserves the credit for having halted the decline in horse breeding which seemed inevitable at that period.

14

The age of the fine, 'blood' Thoroughbred/Trakehner crosses was past. The loss of the First World War and the demands of the Treaty of Versailles brought about a radical change in circumstances and resulted in most of the army being disbanded, so that East Prussian horse breeding lost its biggest customer. Faced with these changed circumstances Count von Lehndorff had to tackle the difficult task of 'modifying' the Trakehner horse. The demand was now for a powerful warmblood horse with a large frame, which stood over a lot of ground and was deep through the girth. The new *Landstallmeister* accomplished this difficult feat in a short time. Going against the advice of his superior, the *Oberlandstallmeister* in Berlin, who considered that the necessary substance should be provided by crossing with Oldenburg and heavy Anglo-Norman stallions, his first move was to sell some of the breeding stock, which (although they were high-class horses) were too light. Increased use of the heavier, though purebred, stallions at the central stud, and a considerable reduction in the number of Thoroughbred stallions, resulted in a rapid and effective increase in bone and substance. The use of stallions with a solid bone structure on light but good quality mares resulted in offspring of the desired build. Good results were obtained in particular from the stallions Ararad, Thronhüter, Saturn, Parsival, Pirat, Waldjunker and Pirol. The stallions Tempelhüter and Jagdheld discussed above were also used, and their influence can still be seen today.

Special mention must also be made of the excellent medium-sized chestnut stallion Dampfross, who was bred on a small farm and came to the central stud in 1923 after standing at Georgenburg. This exceptional stallion produced outstanding results, and stood at Trakehnen until 1934. He left an indelible stamp on the stock at Trakehnen and on East Prussian horse breeding as a whole. The sire line he founded, particularly through his sons Pythagoras and Hyperion, is highly acclaimed in West Germany (see illustrations on pp. 33–4).

We must not leave this period without mentioning the fact that Siegfried, Count von Lehndorff was responsible for breeding most of the important stallions which stood at the central stud, as well as for adding large numbers of excellent broodmares to the herd. Even today the names Poseidon, Pilger, Kupferhammer, Hyperion, Pythagoras, Hirtensang, Polarstern, Bussard, Astor and Tyrann are still remembered by Trakehner breeders everywhere. Most of these stallions were among the horses which fled from Trakehnen to the West in 1944.

The last *Landstallmeister* of Trakehnen, Dr Ernst Ehlert (1931–1944), was an open-minded man who liked going out and meeting people. He gave fatherly advice to the East Prussian breeders, with whom he was very popular. During his term of

(*Above*) Polarstern (foaled 1930), who was by Astor, was used with very good effect on the black Trakehner herd based at the Gurdzen farm. He contributed the bone and substance which was required at that period in the breed's history, at the same time passing on sufficient breed 'type' and quality.

(*Right*) The legendary sire Dampfross (foaled 1916) by Dingo out of Laura by Passvan. After standing initially at Georgenburg, he stood at stud at Trakehnen from 1923 to 1934. This classic stallion has had an enormous influence on Trakehner breeding right up to the present day.

office the size, shape and qualities of the Trakehner horse were those of an all-rounder suitable for use on the land, in the army or for competition (which was already very popular).

In 1932, on the occasion of the celebrations for the 200th anniversary of the founding of the Trakehnen central stud, a life-size bronze statue of the stallion Tempelhüter was unveiled. This statue, which was sculptured by Reinhold Kuebart, is now in Moscow. In 1974 a replica was erected in front of the German Museum of the Horse in Verden-an-der-Aller.

Dr Ehlert stood many successful and famous stallions including Paradox XX, Bussard, Termit, Semper Idem, Creon, Polarstern and Hirtensang. The dark bay stallion Pythagoras, between 1931 and 1944 alone, produced a total of seventy offspring who went on to stand at stud as stallions. Thus under normal circumstances (that is, if he had remained at stud to the end of his life) he would have become Trakehnen's most important stallion. Some of his sons managed to reach safety in the West at the end of the Second World War.

Soon after he had taken up office at Trakehnen, Dr Ehlert set up a fifth herd at Taukenischken for the purpose of bringing in some new blood. In fact he brought in about thirty purebred Arabian, English Thoroughbred and Anglo-Arab mares. In addition to the mares he introduced the Arab stallions Fetysz OX, Lowelas OX and Harun al Raschid OX, whose influence is still very much in evidence.

Successful mare lines developed from this herd, for example the well-known Donau line which traces back to the mare Dongola OX by Jasir OX. These lines have also had considerable influence in West Germany. During Dr Ehlert's term of office the quality of all five herds at the central stud reached a standard which, in the view of authorities on the subject, was unequalled anywhere in the world. The uniformity and trueness to type of each herd were striking, while the individual horses were impressive in their obvious good breeding, their beauty, their harmony and the exemplary correctness of their conformation.

The whole Trakehnen estate comprised by this time an area of approximately 6021 hectares (14,830 acres), of which 2889 hectares (7166 acres) were arable, 1381 hectares (3412 acres) meadowland, 1090 hectares (2696 acres) grassland, 241 hectares (695 acres) tracks, lakes and parkland, 198 hectares (490 acres) woodland, 75 hectares (190 acres) garden and 57 hectares (140 acres) rented. [In Trakehnen, certain areas of grassland were intensively managed – regularly mown, fertilised and possibly irrigated. These are referred to here as 'meadowland'. 'Grassland', on the other hand, was mown once yearly and not fertilised or irrigated.]

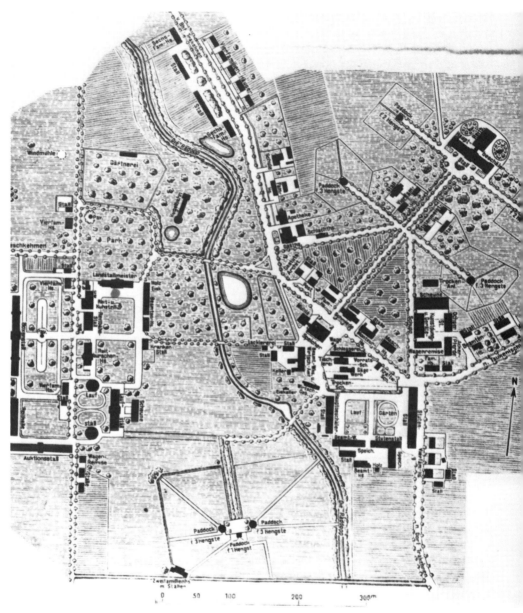

Plan of the main farm at the Trakehnen stud in the 1930s, scale 1:5500. On the left is the Neuer Hof farm. The summer quarters for the stallions are the 'Paddocks' shown in the top right-hand corner and at the bottom.

The central stud consisted of sixteen farms:

Central farm:

> *Trakehnen*: The *Landstallmeister* and the central administration (accountant's office and secretariat). Farm (agricultural) and farm office. Building and maintenance administration and facilities. Medical facilities/pharmacy. Veterinary service. Main feed stores and mill. Master blacksmith. Stallion boxes and paddocks.
>
> *Alter Hof*: Chestnut broodmare herd.
>
> *Neuer Hof*: Hunting stable. Auction stable. Outdoor and indoor schools. Riders' accommodation. Driving stable. Hound kennels. Stabling for weanling colt foals.

Bajohrgallen: Mixed-colour broodmare herd.

Taukenischken: Arab herd.

Gurdzen: Black broodmare herd.

Kalpakin: Bay broodmare herd.

Jonasthal: Herd of heavier broodmares.

Birkenwalde: Horses which failed selection and were to be discarded.

Burgsdorfhof: Quarantine farm.

Danzkehmen: Yearling fillies.

Guddin: Breeding cattle.

Jodzlauken: Two-year-old fillies; sheep.

Mattischkehmen: Yearling colts; sheep.

Neu-Budupönen: Two-year-old colts.

Alt-Budupönen: Breeding cattle.

Alt-Kattenau (former remount depot): Weanling filly foals; breeding cattle.

Neu-Kattenau: Bullocks. Isolation block.

In the whole of the Trakehnen complex there was 1100 head of breeding stock belonging to the central stud, approximately 500 farm horses, approximately 900 head of breeding cattle and bullocks, and approximately 600 sheep and lambs!

Trakehnen prior to its destruction: summary

Trakehnen was the 'sanctuary of the horse', the crowning glory of the Prussian horse-breeding industry. Its fame had spread all over the world.

Much of its success was due to the knowledge, ability and teamwork of all those who worked at the stud. The *Landstallmeister* was in charge, and was assigned two assistants, who were also there to gain further experience in running a stud. The

An example of the ideal combination of quality, substance and superlative paces was the Trakehnen central stud's stallion Pilger, by Luftgott out of Palasthüterin by Tempelhüter. He was born at Trakehnen in 1926. His name stands out on the long list of successful central stud stallions as a sire with outstanding breeding points.

Opposite page, top
There were always several Thoroughbred stallions standing at the Trakehnen central stud. Of these the most influential and prepotent sire in the later years was Paradox XX by Christian de Wet XX, whose influence was felt in the private East Prussian horse-breeding industry as well as at the Trakehnen central stud, where he was foaled in 1919.

Opposite page, bottom
Several purebred Arabians stood at Trakehnen between 1936 and 1944. Of these, the stallion with the most quality was Fetysz OX, foaled in Janow Podlaski in 1924, who was considered the best of his breed in Europe at the time. His line continues to flourish via his grandson Maharadscha.

Landstallmeister's deputy was the longest-serving stud veterinarian. Just before its destruction, there were sixteen stallions standing at Trakehnen. The following is a list of those stallions which set off for the West in the autumn of 1944:

PILGER (foaled 1926), bay, by Luftgott out of Palasthüterin by Tempelhüter
HYPERION (1926), chestnut, by Dampfross out of Hypothese by Haselhorst
PYTHAGORAS (1927), brown, by Dampfross out of Pechmarie by Tempelhüter
BUSSARD (1928), black, by Waldjunker out of Botin by Polarsturm
POLARSTERN (1930), black, by Astor out of Polare by Waldjunker
HIRTENSANG (1930), chestnut, by Parsival out of Hirnschale by Lichtenstein
ALIBI (1932), chestnut, by Parsival out of Alicante by Dampfross
HELLESPONT (1935), bay, by Marduck XX out of Hellebarde by Tempelhüter
PORT ARTHUR (1936), bay, by Pilger out of Porta by Tempelhüter
CREON (1937), bay, by Pythagoras out of Cremona by Ararad
HERR MAJOR (1941), chestnut, by Termit out of Hermione by Helios
AIROLO XX (1931), chestnut, by Teddy XX out of Abbazia XX by Dark Ronald XX
FETYSZ OX (1924), grey, by Bakszysz OX out of Siglavi Bagdady OX by Siglavy Bagdady OX
LOWELAS OX (1930), chestnut, by Koheilan IV-3 OX out of Elegantka OX by Bakszysz OX

All these stallions were evacuated but disappeared in the confusion at the end of the war. Only Polarstern was found, at the beginning of the 1950s, and played an important part in the revival of horse breeding in Poland.

In the summer months the stallions were kept at the various farms with the mare herds, receiving proper handling and exercise daily. Outside the covering season, weather permitting, they lived in their own attractive individual complexes consisting of stables with attached paddocks. Only during the worst of the winter were they kept in the 'stallion boxes', though still going outside daily for exercise. It is clear that this form of management was intended to preserve, as far as organised breeding would permit, the natural lifestyle and habits of the horses. All the horses were handled from when they were foals, and the aim throughout this handling was to make them easy to manage, give them confidence in man, and build up a friendly relationship between man and horse.

Over the centuries, large numbers of stallions passed through Trakehnen. Out of all these sires, relatively few have left their mark, though each of those who have stands out as an equine personality in his own right. These stallions continue to exercise an enormous influence on Trakehner breeding today. For example, several sons of the legendary Pythagoras, of the chestnut Termit, and of Creon and Hirtensang survived the journey to the West. Also, the male line of Fetysz OX has been particularly successful since the 1960s, thanks to the efforts of his descendants, for example Flaneur (see illustration on p. 70).

For decades, the broodmare population at Trakehnen had stood at around 350. At the time of the evacuation, in October 1944, there were 378 mares, all selected in accordance with carefully thought-out plans, and comprising a valuable pool of the finest examples of the various bloodlines to be drawn upon as required. This broodmare stock represented 200 years of work and selection.

As has already been mentioned, Trakehner mares were traditionally kept in five separate herds depending on type, colour and build. The Trakehnen farm housed the chestnut herd, comprising approximately eighty mares; the Bajohrgallen farm had the mixed-colour herd (about seventy mares); the Gurdzen farm had the black herd (seventy-two mares); at Kalpakin was the bay herd (about sixty-five mares). Jonasthal housed the heavy herd (about fifty mares).

The herd of the heavier type of mares at Jonasthal had been formed in 1933, on the instructions of *Oberlandstallmeister* Gustav Rau, by selecting all the heaviest mares from the other herds. The aim was to produce a permanent supply of heavier stallions. These so-called 'support stallions' were to be used to counteract any tendency in the breed to become too light. There was also a herd of thirty purebred Arabians, English Thoroughbreds and Anglo-Arabs at Taukenischken, which had been formed in 1938 by *Landstallmeister* Dr Ehlert with the aim of providing a source of toughness, stamina, top-level performance and high fertility for use at Trakehnen.

Since experience showed that at Trakehnen the foals which were born early were the ones which prospered, it was customary to start covering the mares in the middle of November and to finish by the end of May, so as to ensure as early a foaling as possible. The foals remained with their dams for five months, and were then weaned off into large herds, a colt herd and a filly herd. [This practice of early covering still continues today and significant numbers of Trakehner foals are born in November and December every year.]

Young stallions destined for breeding were broken to saddle in the December of the year in which they were two-and-a-half to three years old and then examined the following May by a selection committee to ascertain whether or not they were

23

In the last twenty years of the Trakehnen central stud's existence the quality of the mare herd reached a standard which was unique in the horse world at that time. The photograph shows Estremadura (1929), by Saturn out of Eider by Thronhüter. She had a very successful stud career, producing several stallions who went on to stand at regional studs; in fact she was one of the most reliable mares in the Gurdzen black herd.

suitable for use as stallions in the provincial state studs. In the century leading up to its destruction, the Trakehnen stud produced around 3500 stallions to stand in the provincial and central studs. Potential broodmares were broken to saddle as three-year-olds, and then broken to harness, so as to prove their usefulness.

Horses unsuitable for breeding, and which were to be sold, were also broken to saddle as three-year-olds, and spent the whole summer hunting in the countryside around Trakehnen, over very varied and very difficult terrain. They were then put up for auction in the autumn. Approximately 350 fences scattered around the Trakehnen complex provided the basis for the famous Trakehnen hunts. The wide expanses of grassland were interrupted by spinnies, fenced ditches and streams, and by the impressive Pissa Canal and the various bridges which crossed it. Training in the hunting field was a requirement and a test for the young horses' subsequent career under saddle. They were cantered over ditches, fences and walls and through streams on a long rein, gradually being asked for more and more until they experienced no difficulty in negotiating the most demanding fences: the bank, the Judenbach river, the various doubles at Jonasthal, Taukenischken and Birkenwalde, the 'Trakehner' (a massive pole in a 4-metre (13-ft) deep ditch) at Hasenwäldchen, and so on. These were jumps which could only be successfully negotiated by horses which threw themselves into their job with boldness and energy, and had a good natural jump. They also had to be able to regain their balance promptly on landing. This rigorous testing produced a batch of first-class performance horses for sale every year. These horses were much sought after by competition riders and spread Trakehnen's fame around the world.

Stutmeister were responsible for the broodmare herds at the various farms. Older *Oberwärter* were usually placed in charge of the young horse herds. They were assisted by *Gestütwärter*. *Stutmeister* and *Oberwärter* were chosen on the basis of their expert knowledge, proficiency, trustworthiness and ability to command respect.

For the horse lover, each farm was of interest in its own right. Very representative of the establishment was the classical-style house occupied by the *Landstallmeister* at the central Trakehnen farm. It stood in an idyllic park full of mature trees. As the visitor approached through the gateway, which was itself of architectural interest, the green parkland in front of the house came into sight, and with it the fine old oak trees and the life-size bronze statue of the stallion Tempelhüter by the sculptor Reinhold Kuebart. Originally this position had been occupied by a bronze effigy of the stallion Morgenstrahl, but this was removed by the Russians in 1914 and taken to Moscow, never to return. The same fate later befell the Tempelhüter statue.

The pleasing grounds of the stud, created by *Landstallmeister* von Oettingen, were a splendid sight. They surrounded and adjoined the new stallion block, the paddocks and 'summer residences' of the stallions, the hunting block, the indoor school, the stables of the horses which were to be sold, the weaning stable, the stable lads' house, the driving stables and the kennels. These buildings, together with adjoining fields and park-like areas with trees dotted around them, comprised the 'Neuer Hof' farm.

The chestnut herd, seen here at the Alter Hof, was of the highest overall quality of any of the Trakehnen stud's five herds. For faithful and reliable hereditary transmission the mares from this herd were among the best at the Trakehnen stud.

The 'Alter Hof' farm at Trakehnen was the site of the over 200-year-old former stallion block, and was also the home of the chestnut broodmare herd, which was always considered to be the finest of them all. Also at 'Alter Hof' was the oldest building at Trakehnen, the simple but very quaint former farmhouse, which was the home of the stud's vet. Tradition has it that Friedrich Wilhelm I, Frederick the Great and Queen Luise stayed there when they visited the stud.

Special mention must be made of the 200-year-old oak trees, which were widely spaced and so had grown into magnificent specimens. They lined the drives which led from Trakehnen, via Bajohrgallen, to Gurdzen and Kalpakin, and from Bajohrgallen to Jonasthal. These mighty giants were reminiscent of a past age. A tour along

26

these beautifully maintained tree-lined drives was an experience in itself. The herds of horses grazed in stoutly railed fields along either side of the drives. On the unfenced areas of meadowland more groups of horses grazed under the supervision of mounted herdsmen.

Hence it was not only the quality of its horses but also its charm and its general harmony which earned Trakehnen the distinction of being, according to authorities on the subject, the most important large stud in the world at that time.

Trakehnen achieved its main aim, which was to produce genetically valuable performance stallions to stand at the provincial studs and so to promote and influence provincial horse breeding. Today's 'Warmblood Horse of Trakehner Origin' is still reaping the benefits of all the work carried out at Trakehnen.

Regional horse breeding

The regional state studs (Landgestüte)

As has already been mentioned, the setting up of the provincial studs was an excellent way for the state to promote horse breeding within its boundaries. For a time there were five provincial studs in East Prussia: Georgenburg, Gudwallen, Braunsberg, Rastenburg and Marienwerder. The *Landgestüt* Gudwallen, however, was disbanded in 1930, and its stallions transferred to Georgenburg.

The stud which played the most important part in provincial horse breeding was without doubt the *Landgestüt* Georgenburg, which lay 3 kilometres (just under 2 miles) north of Insterburg in the same area as the central stud. Founded in 1899, it housed the largest number of stallions as well as the ones which were most valuable for breeding. There were always about 300 stallions in its stables at any one time. In spite of their numbers, these stallions were of very high quality. Each year, when the new stallions were allocated, Georgenburg always received special consideration. It was Georgenburg which supplied the stallions for the Trakehnen area. During the covering season it sent stallions to stand at stations near the towns of Dakehmen, Goldap, Gumbinnen, Insterburg, Niederburg, Pillkallen, Stallupönen and Tilsit, and in Memelland. Most of these stallion stations were also the most important private studs in provincial horse breeding. Sometimes they stood as many as ten state stallions at a time.

The best known private studs were the von Zitzewitz stud at Weedern near Darkehmen, Dr Stahl's stud at Buylien near Gumbinnen, the Krebs stud at Schim-

The homeland and original breeding area of East Prussia, showing the Trakehnen central stud and the Georgenburg, Gudwallen, Rastenburg, Braunsberg and Marienwerder regional studs.

melhof near Darkehmen, the von Sperber stud at Lenken in the Tilsit–Ragnit area, the Voigt stud at Dombrowken near Darkehmen, the Scharffetter stud at Kallwischken near Insterburg and the von Lenski stud at Kattenau near Ebenrode. Even on the small studs the mares were in plentiful supply and of very high quality.

The last director of the Georgenburg stud was *Landstallmeister* Dr Martin Heling. He succeeded in evacuating a large proportion of the stallions to West Germany. Several of these stallions contributed to the birth of Trakehner breeding in West Germany and founded sire lines which are very influential today. Among these were Tropenwald by Termit who founded, through his son Pregel, what is probably the most important line in the West; and Totilas by Pythagoras, who is described as the most prominent foundation stallion in West German Trakehner breeding (see p. 46).

28

The *Landgestüt* Rastenburg was always considered to be the second most important state stud. Founded in 1877, it had a stallion population of about 150, and served
the areas of Angerburg, Bartenstein, Gerdauen, Johannisburg, Lyck, Lötzen, Rastenburg and Sensburg. *Landstallmeister* Dr W. Uppenborn was the last director of
Rastenburg. There were also a number of very important private studs in this region,
among them the von Kuenheim stud at Juditten (Bartenstein), the Graf Rautter stud
at Willkamm (Gerdauen), the von Janson stud at Kinderhof (Gerdauen), the
Freiherr von Schroetter stud at Gross-Wohnsdorff (Bartenstein) and the Plock-
Sechserben stud (Gerdauen). The entire stock of stallions from the Rastenburg stud
was lost during the flight to the West in 1944–1945.

The most uniform and high quality broodmare material was bred in the area
around Treuburg, Lyck and Gerdauen. The most dominant lines, in particular in the
years leading up to the outbreak of war, were those of Astor and Waldjunker, who
had been used to introduce more bone and substance. Consequently the horses bred
in this area were mostly of the heavier type, with big solid frames, sometimes tending
towards coarseness. They were mostly black in colour, eminently suited to work on
the land, as driving and utility horses. International East Prussian competition horses
came from the Rastenburg area. One of these was Fasan, a member of the successful
three-day event team at the 1936 Olympics. The 1936 Olympic champion Nurmi was
born at the Paul stud at Rudwangen near Sensburg (see illustration on p. 77).

The *Landgestüt* Braunsberg, which was founded in 1890, served the area comprising Allenstein, Braunsberg, Fischhausen, Heiligenbeil, Heilsberg, Königsberg,
Labiau, Mohrungen, Preussisch Eylau, Preussisch Holland, Rössel and Wehlau, and
had about 150 stallions. Among the well-known and successful studs in this area were
those of Freiherr von der Goltz at Kallen (Fischhausen), Rodde at Kattern (Mohrungen), Finck at Ziegenberg (Fischhausen), von Siegfried at Karben (Heiligenbeil),
von Saint Paul at Jaecknitz (Heiligenbeil), Gutsverwaltung Borken at Preussisch
Eylau, von Kobylinski at Korbsdorf (Braunsberg) and Count zu Stolberg-Wernige-
rode at Dönhoffstaedt (Rastenburg).

The last *Landstallmeister* at Braunsberg stud was H. W. von Warburg. He
successfully evacuated most of the stallions, on foot, to central Germany. However,
most of them then fell into the hands of the occupying powers, although a few very
valuable stallions did finally reach West Germany.

Especially in the Preussisch Holland, Mohrungen, Fischhausen and Heiligenbeil
areas, the mares owned by the local farmer-breeders were of very high quality. Near
Georgenburg there were numerous stallions descended from the highly esteemed

29

There was a special magic about the East Prussian countryside with its lush meadows, its ancient trees, and its buildings which were so well integrated with their rural surroundings. Here, with expert management, the Warmblood Horse of Trakehner Origin thrived and developed its legendary toughness.

'Löwe–Markeur' line, which was popular there and had many branches. From these stallions the local stock inherited substance and energetic, ground-covering paces.

The Mohrungen area was the home of one of the oldest breeding and rearing establishments of the quality East Prussian horse, the Schlobitten and Prökelwitz estates, which belonged to the Prince of Dohna. The centuries old, consolidated female lines bred and developed at this stud almost all reached safety in West Germany, and greatly influenced present-day Trakehner breeding. Ararad's son Indra stood in 1944 at a stallion station at Prökelwitz and produced some important female offspring which were successfully evacuated. He himself was left behind and lost.

The *Landgestüt* Marienwerder was established in 1788. After Trakehnen it was the oldest stud in East Prussia. In the years leading up to the war it stood about seventy warmblood stallions, and served the Elbing, Marienburg, Marienwerder, Neidenburg, Ortelsburg, Osterode, Rosenberg and Stuhm area. From 1930 onwards Marienwerder was under the control of *Landstallmeister* Ehlers. In his zone the Perfectionist XX line predominated, via Tempelhüter, and even more so via his brother Irrlehrer, whose entire stock was at Marienwerder for a time. The most important private stud in the area was the Gutsverwaltung Finckenstein, near Rosenberg, which had over forty broodmares.

In the twenty years before the flight in 1944, there were about 20,000 warmblood mares registered in the stud book of the breed association, the *Ostpreussische Stutbuchgesellschaft*. Hence East Prussia had by far the largest horse-breeding industry in Germany. In 1937 alone, 35,000 mares were covered by stallions from regional studs! All the farmers used to bring their mares, usually two to five in number, to these stallions, which stood at centrally located stallion stations. Each station had between two and ten stallions, which were based there from February until the end of June, when they returned to the regional stud.

The Ostpreussische Stutbuchgesellschaft

The three things which did most to promote East Prussian horse breeding were the setting up of the central and regional studs, the enactment of the stallion licensing order and the formation of a breeders' association by the private breeders. This *Ostpreussische Stutbuchgesellschaft für Warmblut Trakehner Abstammung* (East Prussian Stud Book Association for Warmbloods of Trakehner Origin) was founded relatively late, in 1888, and had its headquarters in Königsberg. Only horses which had proven pure, unbroken lineage were accepted for registration. The registered mares were of universally high quality.

At first the breed association's primary concern was to register the broodmares. This was carried out in collaboration with the *Landstallmeisters* of the various studs. After the First World War, with the agreement of the Prussian breed authorities and the chambers of agriculture, various new measures were introduced for the promotion of horse breeding. The responsibility for carrying out these measures was placed in the hands of eminent authorities who were presidents of the association and themselves important breeders. Names such as von Zitzewitz (Weedern), Freiherr von der Schroetter (Gross-Wohnsdorff) and Dr Fritz Schilke will always be remembered in connection with the history of the East Prussian Warmblood of Trakehner Origin. In 1947, the *Ostpreussische Stutbuchgesellschaft für Warmblut Trakehner Abstammung* was disbanded. In its place the *Verband der Züchter und Freunde des Warmblutpferdes Trakehner Abstammung e.V. – Trakehner Verband* (Society of breeders and friends of the warmblood horse of Trakehner origin – Trakehner society) was set up with its headquarters at Hamburg.

As has already been mentioned, horse breeding in East Prussia was mostly in the hands of farmers. There were only about twenty studs with more than twenty registered mares. It is interesting to note that the farmer-breeders mostly disposed of the foals at weaning to studs which specialised in rearing youngstock. At these centres they were kept and prepared for the stallion licensing or for presentation to the remount committee. Auctions were held yearly, in Königsberg, Insterburg, Marienburg and other provincial towns. At these sales, mature working horses and competition horses changed hands.

From 1920 onwards, the best products of East Prussian warmblood breeding were sent to 'Green Week', an exhibition organised by the *Deutsche Landwirtschafts-Gesellschaft* (DLG: German Agricultural Society) and held in Berlin. Held in conjunction with this event was the famous exhibition of East Prussian horses and an auction run by the East Prussian chamber of agriculture, all of which was organised by the eminent authority on horses, Hugo Steinberg. East Prussian horses sold at this event realised above-average prices. Even after the destruction of the stud, horses of Trakehner origin were always the most sought after and stallions, broodmares and saddle horses were exported all over the world, going as far afield as Japan, Australia, South Africa and the USSR.

Important male lines

Since horse breeding on a regional level was originally aimed mainly at producing remounts for the army, and so at promoting those qualities which were desirable in a riding horse, a certain class of stallion soon emerged which had an above-average tendency to pass on riding horse qualities.

In the forefront was Pirol who during his period at stud produced 258 remounts for the army. Then came Salut, who sired 251 remounts, Erzengel (238), and Bulgarenzar (225). The stallions Draufgänger, Salvator, Wellenschlag, Marke, Markant and Held each sired over 200 offspring which satisfied the remount committee's rigorous selection criteria.

The male line of the chestnut Dampfross and his numerous sons stands out especially as being particularly good for transmitting riding qualities. Stallions from this line were much sought after by all the regional studs and were highly esteemed in East Prussia. Dampfross himself was used both in the central stud and on a regional level. He rose to fame in particular as the sire of numerous licensed stallions. He had a striking ability to pass on to his progeny presence, sturdy, correct conformation and excellent ground-covering, energetic, elastic paces. His descendants were also much appreciated as riding horses on account of their easy, even and generous temperaments. In all about fifty of his sons served at East Prussian regional studs. His influence was spread even wider by his numerous grandchildren and great-grandchildren.

Dampfross's sons Pythagoras and Hyperion, who have already been discussed, had very successful careers as stallions at the Trakehnen central stud, as did Hyperion's son Termit, whose progeny Abglanz and Pregel are among the most successful riding horse sires and founders of sire lines in the history of German warmblood

The brown Pythagoras, born at Trakehnen in 1927, by Dampfross out of Pechmarie by Tempelhüter, would have been the most influential and important stallion ever used at Trakehnen if he had stood there until the end of his days. The evacuation of the stud in the autumn of 1944 put a premature end to his career.

Hyperion (foaled 1926), by Dampfross out of Hypothese by Haselhorst, was a prepotent stallion who stood at the central Trakehnen stud until 1944 but was lost during the flight to the West.

Ararad (foaled 1921), a black son of Jagdheld was a stallion with substance and long lines who can claim the rare honour of having spent his entire life at stud at Trakehnen. He earned this through his extremely effective prepotency. Numerous sons of his stood at regional studs. His stock inherited substance and outstanding paces, as well as a pleasing 'type'.

Opposite page, bottom
An important son of the legendary Thoroughbred stallion Perfectionist XX was Jagdheld, born at Trakehnen in 1906, out of Jagdfreundin by Optimus. He stood at the central stud from 1918 until 1929, and produced outstanding hunters and performance horses.

breeding. Looking back over the years, the Dingo–Dampfross line can be seen to be one of the most important in the development of the breed.

Other very important stallions based at the regional studs were Eichendorf, Eklatant, Hexenschuss, Immer Voran and Semper Idem, whose influence is still felt today in West German Trakehner breeding. Semper Idem founded one of the great sire lines in postwar Hanoverian breeding, whilst Immer Voran is a particularly prominent name in Swedish warmblood breeeding.

The most dominant line in East Prussian breeding is that of the English Thoroughbred Perfectionist XX. This exceptionally prepotent stallion founded a male line which plays a major role today in German riding horse breeding. His sons Tempelhüter, Jagdheld and Irrlehrer, who have already been mentioned, were born at the central Trakehnen stud. Of these, the brown Tempelhüter was the most influential, producing nearly seventy stallions and over sixty broodmares for the Trakehnen herds, until he was finally put down in 1932 on account of old age. However, his brother Jagdheld surpassed him in passing on performance qualities, siring numerous highly talented riding horses which were successful in top level sport. The Jagdheld branch, via Ararad–Hutten–Humboldt–Impuls, has assumed even more significance in West German Trakehner breeding than the Tempelhüter line. Ararad in particular was, during his lifetime, one of the central stud's most consistent stallions. He produced good stallions for regional horse breeding, and numerous broodmares with bone and substance.

Tempelhüter was the sire of many of the best broodmares at Trakehnen. Among these were Technik (the dam of numerous stallions including the central stud stallion Termit), Palasthüterin and Kronhüterin (dams of the central stud stallions Pilger and Kupferhammer respectively). Tempelhüter's sons Indogermane, Lustig, Pirat, Sandor and Thronhüter, among others, saw to it that his qualities were preserved for posterity. Horses bred from the Perfectionist XX line proved themselves to be extremely tough in the yearly stallion performance testing sessions, and were also extraordinarily successful in top-level competition.

The third most important male line overall in East Prussian breeding is probably that of Obelisk, via his sons Charm and Lichtenstein. Horses descended from this bloodline were very popular in regional horse breeding, as well as being sought after by the remount committee. They were characterised by their bone, their correct joints, their good depth of girth and their robust build. They often tended towards coarseness, but they were ideal for crossing with high-class, very highly bred mares. Charm's son Fahnenträger went to the Celle stud in 1934 when he was quite advanced in years, and even so had considerable success there. Only a few representatives of the Obelisk line reached the sanctuary of West Germany. The valuable male line is now extinct.

Another important male line which is worthy of mention is that of Padorus. In the last years of Trakehnen's existence the Padorus line, via his sons Skat, Skatbruder and Markeur, had gained quite a foothold in East Prussia. Descendants of this line,

The progeny of Hirtensang by Parsival all inherited outstanding 'type', together with substance and dynamic paces. Hirtensang, who was foaled in 1930 at Trakehnen, was an important sire in the history of Trakehnen's chestnut herd. Through his sons and his daughters he has had a profound and widespread influence on West German Trakehner breeding.

especially the Markeur branch, were typical examples of the large-framed, rather heavy East Prussian horse with plenty of bone and excellent, powerful, elastic paces.

Padorus' grandson Löwe was famous for producing not only broodmares with substance and depth of girth but also numerous quality stallions to stand at the regional studs, in particular Georgenburg. The famous Kallwischken stud, owned by Franz Scharffetter, enjoyed enormous success as a result of combining the blood of the highly bred Dampfross with that of the coarser and heavier products of the Löwe line. The well-known Julmond, who went to West Germany and is known as the 'reformer of Württemberg warmblood breeding' (in which his male line still survives today), was a product of this line.

In the very last years, the smaller sire lines of Parsival, Waldjunker and Astor became increasingly important in East Prussia. They still play an important role in West German Trakehner breeding.

Even though there were certain differences in weights and shape from one sire line to another, the warmbloods bred in East Prussia were of a distinct, set type. The mares were on average 156 to 162 cm high (15.2 to 16 hands), with a girth measurement of 180 to 200 cm (70 to 79 inches). They were supposed to have not less than 19 cm (8 inches) of bone below the knee. For stallions a height of 160 to 166 cm (15.3 to 16.1½ hands) was desirable, with a girth measurement of 190 to 200 cm (75 to 79 inches) and 21 to 22 cm (8½ to 8¾ inches) of bone below the knee. Both mares and stallions were to be broad and deep through the body, must never be 'on the leg' or flat-ribbed, must have a ground-covering walk and a powerful, elastic trot, and must always be clean-limbed and full of quality.

Nowadays, although the type and breed characteristics of the Trakehner are still retained, the change in market demands has resulted in an increase in height. A height of 160 to 165 cm (15.3 to 16.1 hands) is now desirable in mares, and 162 to 168 cm (16 to 16.2 hands) in stallions.

East Prussian horse breeding was devastated and its foundations destroyed when it was a its peak. The *Stutbuchgesellschaft* had 13,883 members in 1944, and its books contained 852 living stallions in the stallion register, and 26,264 living broodmares in the broodmare register.

3 The development of Trakehner breeding in West Germany

The evacuation

During the months of July, August and September 1944 the signs of an impending Russian invasion of eastern Germany became more and more difficult to ignore. Every evening the eastern sky was reddened by fires and explosions. The director of the central stud began to consider evacuation. The first thought was for the valuable equine breeding stock, about 1100 in all, although there was also an inestimable worth of working horses, cattle, foodstuffs and so on.

Landstallmeister Dr Ehlert's prompt, repeated requests to *Gauleiter* Koch for a permit to remove the breeding stock were rejected in Königsberg. A large number of elderly people were then evacuated to Saxony. Shortly afterwards the thunder of cannons was heard. This was followed by night-time air raids on Tilsit and Insterburg. Up to this point, however, Trakehnen had been spared, but from then on matters continued to come to a head. At the beginning of September, Dr Ehlert finally obtained a permit to evacuate the central stud's stallions and 'some' of the best in-foal mares. On his own initiative he increased the number of mares destined for the journey to a total of 139. On 11 September 1944, thirty-four two-year-old stallions were distributed among the regional studs. On 15 September fifty-eight yearling colts were evacuated to Hunnesrück, and sixty weanling colts and seventy-nine fillies were loaded up to be taken to the regional stud at Labes (Pomerania). The military authorities still refused to authorise the evacuation of the 700 or so horses which remained. The fears of the staff at the stud grew as continuous streams of refugees and large herds of cattle filed through the region. On 16 October 1944 it became obvious that the invasion was imminent.

On 17 October 1944, on the orders of the Ebenrode divisional command, the general evacuation of the twelve farms of the Trakehnen stud in the Ebenrode area was set in motion. According to instructions, the four farms which belonged to the Gumbinnen area were not to be evacuated until 20 October 1944. In spite of these instructions, the breeding stock from these farms set off for Georgenburg on 17 October. The journey had to take place on foot at a non-stop trot, using minor roads, since the main road was blocked. The railway could no longer be used. Hence most of the groups made their own way towards Georgenburg. The stud horses were divided up into ten herds for the march. Each herd contained about eighty horses, and was accompanied by only three escorts, consisting of *Gestütwärter* aged over sixty-five and stable boys under the age of sixteen. Because this number of escorts was totally inadequate, the entire journey to Georgenburg had to be accomplished at a steady trot, without stopping. They arrived there at about six o'clock in the evening, having spent about six hours on the road and covered about 60 or 70 kilometres (about 40 miles). Only one young mare was lost, as the result of serious injury, and according to reports hardly any of the mares or foals showed any signs of lameness.

In Georgenburg, the stock of the Trakehnen stud was divided up into groups for the next stage. *Landstallmeister* Dr Ehlert remained in Georgenburg with the staff of the stud until the breeding stock had been loaded on to railtrucks for the next stage of the journey. They were to be evacuated to different destinations. Dr Ehlert then went to the *Landgestüt* Labes (Pomerania). The farm livestock trekked onwards on 24 October 1944 from Georgenburg to Grosswohnsdorff, where it halted for two days. On 27 October it proceeded to the Preussisch Eylau area where, under the leadership of *Oversattelmeister* Kiaulehn from Trakehnen, it was split up and distributed over the area. In the middle of January 1945, the advance of the Russians forced it to move on again over the ice of the bay of Frisches Haff to Danzig. Many parts of the convoy were left behind in West Prussia and Pomerania, but a few small groups managed to get through to western Germany. Those which were left behind fell into the hands of either the Russians or the Poles.

Because of the advance of the Russian troops, the yearlings and the administration section (secretariat and accountancy) which had been evacuated in the autumn of 1944 to Labes were obliged to move on. In the meantime, negotiations between *Oberlandstallmeister* Dr Seyffert and the military authorities over the use by the stud of a remount depot had been successful. This would enable the stud to be run in an organised fashion. Accordingly, at the beginning of December 1944, the Trakehner stud administration was able to move to Perlin (Mecklenburg). By the middle of December a total of 290 horses had been transferred there. These comprised 139 breeding animals from Silesia, 112 from Labes, 39 from Graditz and 17 working horses. However, before long the bases in Silesia to which horses had been evacuated were under threat from the advancing front. The convoy from Berbisdorf, which set out on 16 February 1945, took until 4 March to reach the central stud at Graditz, having sustained heavy losses. The Trakehners which were evacuated to Neustadt were lost to the Russians a few weeks later. The 140 horses evacuated to Graditz and the thirteen Trakehner broodmares and eleven central stud stallions which arrived there on 4 March 1945 from Berbisdorf also fell into the hands of the Russians.

Their journey to the West had been hindered by American occupation forces. After a high-ranking British officer had intimated to *Landstallmeister* Dr Ehlert that a Russian occupation of Perlin was possible, it was obvious that evacuation to the West would have to be considered. The plan was rejected by the English authorities, but the English general concerned issued a pass for thirty-six horses and the necessary escorts, so that on 30 June 1945 two central stud stallions, twenty-eight Trakehner mares and six foals were able to move to Ratzeburg in Holstein.

The *Oberpräsident* (governor) of Schleswig-Holstein requested the secretary of the *Ostpreussischen Stutbuchgesellschaft* (East Prussian breed society), Dr Schilke, to deal with these horses, and on 1 October 1947 twenty-two original Trakehner mares from this group passed by deed of sale into the ownership of what was later to become the Trakehner *Verband* (Trakehner Society). By contrast, on 31 August 1945 the remounts and 278 horses from the Trakehnen central stud's stock had been loaded on to trains and taken to Russia, so very few of the original stock found their way to established homes in the West.

In the autumn of 1944 the East Prussian private breeders had already begun evacuating their animals. Those in the eastern districts of Goldap, Pillkallen, Gumbinnen and Ebenrode were the first to leave, because these were the areas which first succumbed to the Russian invasion. Only those which, harnessed to waggons, survived the rigours of winter and the air raids managed to reach the safety of the West. This journey was the toughest ever performance test in the history of horse breeding. Most of the broodmares were in foal, and food supplies were strictly rationed, especially bulk foods.

When, in 1945, the Russian troops suddenly surrounded East Prussia, the civilian population began to flee to the West. Soon the only route to safety was over the frozen Frisches Haff bay and along the narrow strip of land known as Frische Nehrung. This part of the journey was described by all who took part as the most dangerous and exhausting. Many of the evacuees reached central Germany, only to fall into the hands of the occupying powers as the Russians advanced.

In the spring of 1945 about 1500 purebred broodmares arrived in the area which is now West Germany. After their weeks of hardship, a large proportion of these were then also lost, either through requisitioning or slaughter. In this part of Germany, East Prussian refugees counted as intruders, and there was no longer any means of support for the broodmares. Consequently in 1947 only about 700 registered brood-

The expressive heads of two original Trakehner mares: the grey Kassette (foaled 1937), by Harun al Raschid OX out of Kasematte by Flieder, was the founder of the largest mare family in West Germany; on the right Polarfahrt (foaled 1940), black, by Bussard out of Polarluft by Astor, who was the winning mare at the German Agricultural Society (DLG) show on two occasions, and whose valuable, centuries-old bloodlines continue to exert an enormous influence on Trakehner breeding today.

mares and about 60 regional stud stallions, predominantly from the Georgenburg regional stud, were available to start a new breeding programme. No foals were born in 1946 or 1947, so 1948 was the first full season for the breed in its new home.

New beginnings

When the home of the breed, the province of East Prussia, was lost to the Russians at the end of the Second World War in the spring of 1945, the breeding of the East

Prussian Warmblood of Trakehner Origin seemed to have suffered irretrievable damage, and its history to have drawn to a close. It seemed impossible that with the central stud and the work of 18,000 breeders destroyed, what had been the largest and highest quality horse-breeding industry in the world could continue in existence. The loss was incalculable, and the figures alone do not convey the full extent of the tragedy. Out of the 26,264 mares and 852 stallions which were registered in 1944 in the *Stutbuch für Warmblut Trakehner Abstammung* (Studbook for Warmbloods of Trakehner Origin) and used for breeding, there remained only a pitiful 700 mares and 60 stallions, and these were scattered all over West Germany. Yet with typical East Prussian perseverance, the breeding of the Warmblood of Trakehner Origin was revived.

This revival, from the most difficult beginnings, and the subsequent dramatic growth in Trakehner breeding, which still continues today, are unique in the history of animal breeding.

A considerable amount of work obviously went into this success story, especially in view of the chaotic conditions of the postwar period. Siegfried Freiherr von Schroeter and Dr Fritz Schilke, the chairman and the secretary of the *Ostpreussische Stutbuchgesellschaft*, collected and identified the horses, and in 1947 founded the *Verband der Züchter und Freunde des Warmblutpferdes Trakehner Abstammung e.V.*, or Trakehner *Verband* for short, which had its headquarters in Hamburg. This organisation brought together all the breeders and the many friends of the Trakehner horse. It ensured the continuation of Trakehner breeding along the traditional, tried and tested lines, and so preserved the oldest live cultural asset of eastern Germany.

Three further people played an essential part in the reconstruction and the shaping of Trakehner breeding and of the Trakehner *Verband*: they were Dietrich von Lenski, Andreas Peter, Count von Bernstorff and Ulrich Poll. They remained on the committee of the Trakehner *Verband* for many years.

Among the mares registered in the newly opened stud book were eighteen which had been salvaged from the Trakehnen central stud. They were distributed among the newly created studs at Hunnesrück (Einbeck, Lower Saxony), Schmoel and Rantzau (both in the Plön district of East Holstein). The mares from the central stud were justifiably considered to be the most valuable of the female breeding stock. These three studs, together with the Trakehner Society's *Verbandgestüt* Birkhausen (which has been operating near Zweibrücken in the Pfalz since 1960), have always attached special importance to these bloodlines because they have some of the best and most successful breeding points.

Purebred Trakehner horses are now bred in all the regions of West Germany. The Trakehner *Verband* has a branch in each region and a central office which coordinates the breeding programme. The Trakehners are classed as a 'special breed' by the German Horse Society, the *Deutsche Reiterliche Vereinigung*, which is the umbrella organisation for all the societies representing horse breeding and horse sports. The 'special breeds' category also includes the English Thoroughbred and the Arab, which are also bred on a national level. This subject will be dealt with in more detail later in the book.

	Mares	*Stallions*	*Members*
1949	797	64	515
1959	685	49	642
1969	1530	153	1525
1979	4490	308	3610

The growth of Trakehner breeding from 1949 to 1979

The setting up of breeding zones

Trakehner horses are now bred in all the regions of West Germany. This means that there are Trakehner studs spread all over the country [as opposed to the German regional horse breeds such as the Hanoverian, which are bred only in their region of origin]. The Trakehner *Verband* established nine breeding zones, whose boundaries corresponded more or less to those of the West German states.

Schleswig-Holstein breeding zone

Schleswig-Holstein, Germany's most northern state, is considered to be the nerve centre of West German Trakehner breeding. Most of the East Prussian private breeders, with their waggons pulled by their broodmares, ended their journey in Schleswig-Holstein and took up residence there. In the postwar years the most successful studs, and the first important ones, which are now famous, were in this region.

The Gutswervaltung Schmoel stud (Panker) was established in 1946 in the Plön district by the Kurhessisch foundation, with a number of the finest quality original Trakehner mares, together with other mares bought from private East Prussian breeders. The first stallions at Schmoel were Goldregen, born in 1943 at Trakehnen and sired by Creon, and Famulus, born in 1938 at Trakehnen, sired by Fetysz OX. Many stallions from Schmoel have had considerable influence on West German Trakehner breeding, for example Goldregen's son Komet, and Komet's son Gunnar.

The policy of the Kurhessisch foundation has always been, and still is, to breed from mares of the best bloodlines including those of Herbstzeit by Bussard (Trakehnen central stud), Isola Longa by Tyrann (Trakehnen central stud), Tapete by Pythagoras (Trakehnen central stud), and Blitzrot by Hirtensang (Trakehnen central stud).

The second private stud which has left its mark on Trakehner breeding is the Rantzau Trakehner stud in the Plön district. This stud cultivates the female lines of the original Trakehner mares Kassette by Harun al Raschid OX and Polarfahrt by Bussard, and the line of Donna by Cancara, who was bred by Curt Krebs at Schimmelhof. An outstanding line was also founded at Rantzau by the legendary Schwalbe by Totilas (bred by the Prince of Dohna-Schlobitten) who was champion of the DLG (German Agricultural Society) show. She had nineteen foals, and her line was of great importance for the future of the breed. One of the most important stallions who left his mark on the breed and who stood at Rantzau was Pythagoras' son Totilas, rightfully described as the foundation stallion of West German Trakehner breeding. Some other stallions who stood were Magnet by Pregel, Habicht by Burnus, and the English Thoroughbred Traumgeist XX by Goody.

These two studs produced numerous young stallions which went on to stand at stallion stations all over West Germany, and high-class young broodmares who founded new studs. Many East Prussian breeders and their families found a new home in Schleswig-Holstein, and carried on there the old breeding traditions of their East Prussian homeland. Among those worthy of mention are Hans-Werner Paul (Rethwisch, near Preetz), Erdmuthe von Zitzewitz (Katharinental) and Gerhard Jaeschke (Fresendorf). Further studs which are of interest are the particularly successful Neversfelde stud of Veronika von Schöning where the noted mare Tannenmeise, by Sterndeuter, was bred; Hohenschmark near Malente, and Rondeshagen (Elke Buck von Lingelsheim), which have had considerable success in breeding competition horses; the Neuwetterade stud (Franz Lage); Hans-Christian Först's

Totilas, born at the Trakehnen central stud in 1938, by Pythagoras out of Tontaube by Pilger, contributed over 100 registered mares and was a foundation stallion of West Germany's Trakehner breeding programme.

In the postwar period one of the most productive broodmares, with the most reliable hereditary transmission, was the Totilas mare Schwalbe (foaled 1952). In twenty seasons she produced nineteen foals, and had an enormous influence on the whole breeding programme through her licensed sons Schwärmer, Schwarm and Schwalbenfürst and her daughter Schwarze Schwalbe.

The chestnut mare Tannenmeise (foaled 1967) by Sterndeuter out of Tanjana by Abendstern is a full sister to the stallions Tannenberg, Tannenfels, Tannensee and Tannengrund. She was a top prizewinner at championship level and at other shows. She won the 'Ia-Preis' (best horse in age group) in her class at the first national riding horse show (*Bundesschau des Deutschen Reitpferdes*) in 1979. Bred by Veronika von Schöning, Neversfelde and owned by Ulrich Gorlo, Bielefeld.

stud at Sören, Gottfried Maracke at Pohlsee, Heinrich Ernst at Gut Altenrade and Gerhard Hirsch at Grammdorf.

In 1979 there were forty Trakehner stallions and 800 broodmares in Schleswig-Holstein Trakehner studs.

Lower Saxony/Hanover breeding zone

Because it covers such a large area, Lower Saxony has been divided up for Trakehner breeding purposes into the Lower Saxony/Hanover and Lower Saxony/North West zones. The Lower Saxony/Hanover zone comprises the administrative districts of

47

One of the Trakehner *Verband*'s most successful broodmares was the chestnut Griseldis (1964), by Pindar XX out of Grete by Abendstern. She won the 'Ia-Preis' at the DLG show in Hanover in 1972, was the winning mare at the first national Trakehner breeding stock show in Verden in 1975, and produced four licensed stallions including Grimsel by Kassio. Bred by Dr G. Baronin von Lotzbeck, Mammendorf and owned by the Wiedenhof Stud, Jesteburg.

Hanover, Lüneburg, Hildesheim and West Berlin. Here, in 1946, in the home of the Hanoverian breed, as had happened at the Schmoel (Panker) and Rantzau studs in Schleswig-Holstein, a herd of East Prussian mares of Trakehner origin and three stallions were installed at the state-owned Hünnesruck stud. The mares came mostly from former East Prussian private breeders, but there were some original Trakehnen mares among them. Hünnesruck has been most successful in fulfilling its intended purpose, which was to produce stallions as a basis for building up the Trakehner breed and to cultivate and preserve valuable female lines. The stallions Pregel, Stern

The chestnut mare Kassiopeia (1959), by Impuls out of Kassandra by Sporn, shows to what extent frame size and substance can be increased without loss of type and breed characteristics. She was bred by Fritz Bähre at the Webelsgrund stud and owned by Otto Langels, Hämelschenburg. Among her progeny were the important stallions Kastilio, Kastor and Kassiber.

XX, Hansakapitän, Hessenstein, Altan, Schwalbenflug and Maigraf XX stood at Hunnesrück. These stallions spent only a part of their careers at Hünnesruck, and have had a profound effect on the future of the Trakehner breed as a whole. A stallion of the younger generation who founded a valuable line was Impuls. This stallion had a considerable influence on the development of the Lower Saxony private Trakehner studs at Webelsgrund near Springe and Hamelschenburg near Hamelin. Impuls stood at Webelsgrund into a ripe old age, and the stud was responsible for promoting this valuable bloodline. Webelsgrund was also very successful in the field of young stallion production, and had a herd of first-class broodmares of the large-framed type with plenty of substance, of whom Impuls' daughter Kassiopeia is a prime example. At Hämelschenburg the bay stallion Ibikus was very successful as a sire of licensed stallions and high-class riding horses during the early part of his long career. This stud was also very successful in equestrian competition.

From the outset, a proportion of the private breeders were themselves of East Prussian origin, for example Hans Steinbrück at Gilde, Ulrich and Hubertus Poll at Hörem, Erich Voigt at Dumstorf, Gerhard Gunia at Uslar and Kurt Rosenau at Brunstein. The Medingen monastery near Bad Bevensen has, in addition to a stallion station and a broodmare herd, the only private stallion testing centre in Germany. About sixty to eighty three-year-old stallions are tested every year at this centre. Special mention must also be made of Klaus Rosdorff's stud at Klingenhagen, concentrating on mares from an old and highly esteemed East Prussian bloodline, and the Wiedenhof Trakehner stud at Jesteburg, which was established in the 1970s and by the early 1980s had the largest stallion station in Lower Saxony. This stud is high on the list of important Trakehner studs on account of the high quality of its broodmare herd and its highly rated stallions.

The 1979 German hunter championship in Münster-Handorf was won by the bay stallion Tümmler, ridden by Martin Plewa, and bred by the Schmoel stud.

An example of an exceptional mare is the bay Tamsel, by Schwärmer out of Tanjana by Abendstern, bred by Veronika von Schöning, Neversfelde in 1973. She is half-sister to the stallion Tannenberg. Apart from being used at stud, she has won numerous showing classes.

In 1979 there was a total of 613 registered Trakehner broodmares and thirty-three Trakehner stallions (two of which were at the Celle state stud) in this breeding zone.

Lower Saxony/North West breeding zone

The Lower Saxony/North West breeding zone comprises the Hanse town of Bremen and the administrative districts of Oldenburg and Stade. In this area in particular East Prussian immigrants have had considerable influence on Trakehner breeding, for example the Scharffetter family, which was formerly based at Kallwischken and settled at Brundorf and Ritterhude, near Bremen. This stud was the birthplace of the famous stallion Impuls, who came from stock produced by East Prussian breeders. Impuls left an indelible mark on Trakehner breeding. Dietrich von Lenski, formerly of Kattenau and then of Ritterhude, founded a female line of great quality and character with his grey mare Elfe by Adamas OX, who had survived the journey from East Prussia. This line has produced important competition horses and breeding stock. Peter Elxnant, of Hohenkirchen, also bred from a female line founded by a mare he had brought over from East Prussia. This was the black mare Schwindlerin. There are also well-known Trakehner studs at Bremen-Tenever, Querenstede, Ganderkesee and Volkmarst. In 1979 there were nine Trakehner stallions and 207 broodmares in this zone.

Westphalian breeding zone

The North Rhine/Westphalia area has more horses and riders than any other region of Germany, and is dividied up into the Westphalian and the Rhineland breeding zones. The Westphalian zone comprises the administrative districts of Münster, Detmold and Arnsberg.

This area too received its share of East Prussian settlers, who laid the foundations of what is today a flourishing Trakehner breeding industry in the homeland of the Westphalian Warmblood. The studs of the Schlegel family (Detmold) and the Igor-Meyhöffer family (Detmold), so successful in recent years, had already become the focus of attention in the 1950s. They were joined in the 1960s by the larger studs of the Ellermann family at Brockhagen, the Gorlo family at Bielefeld, the Landwehrmann family at Jöllenbeck and the Brune family at Bielefeld. Stallion stations were also established. All these studs cultivated and successfully preserved the very best female lines; the Schlegel family using the Ilona line, which produced the famous dressage horse Illusion (see p. 85), who was partnered by Harry Boldt. The Igor-Meyhöffer stud's mares are descended from Kavallerie by Lindequist. Kavallerie had survived the journey from East Prussia at the end of the war. In Westphalia, in the heart of the homeland of the Westphalian Warmblood, the number of Trakehner horses has remained relatively low. In 1979 there were 117 registered broodmares and fourteen stallions.

Rhineland breeding zone

Rhineland has more Trakehners registered with the society than any other zone except Schleswig-Holstein. This relatively high level of Trakehner breeding is partially due to the fact that the Trakehner played a predominant role in the development of the modern, postwar Rhinelander horse.

As far back as 1947, the Hoogen family at Vogelsangshof, Kevelaer II, was one of the first to develop a close association with the Trakehner. It was they who acquired the famous chestnut mare Marke, one of the best types of mare to survive the flight to the West. She founded an important line which still survives today, not only at the Vogelsangshof stud. She is represented all over West Germany by stallions and first-class broodmares. Vogelsangshof is the location of one of the largest private stallion stations in Germany, where the stallions are all characterised by their exceptionally high quality, and by their outstanding prepotency which has enabled them to leave their mark on the stock of many smaller studs. A select herd of about fifteen top-quality broodmares of impeccable breeding is also kept. Apart from the Marke line discussed above, the stud has also cultivated the Preussentahne line, which has produced horses such as the Olympic medal winner Perkunos.

There are other studs which have occupied prominent positions in Rhineland Trakehner breeding in recent years, such as the Alpen stud belonging to the Haasler family, who were very well known in East Prussia. This family breeds with most successful results (especially in competition) from descendants of the mares Sylvia, Salve and Wolga, who came from East Prussia at the end of the war.

Karl Schmitz of Burg Dreiborn, Korioth of Monschau and Nesseler of Aachen, all also of East Prussian descent, influenced the development of Trakehner breeding for many years, not only in Rhineland but also in other parts of Germany. The popular stallion stations at the Rittergut Schick riding centre at Enzen and Burg Miel at Swisstal have also been outstandingly successful at bringing out home-bred horses in competitions over the years. Dr Reimer, at Hückeswagen, stood the famous Flaneur (p. 70), belonging to Frau I. I. Wenzel. Flaneur is one of the stallions who has done most to influence postwar Trakehner breeding, having founded one of the most important modern sire lines. There are many licensed stallions by Flaneur standing at stud. These stallions reliably pass on good breeding and riding qualities. More recently established Trakehner studs which have proved successful are those of the Heitfeld and Heinen families at Bönninghardt, the Matthaiwe and van Dreweldt

A modern example of a top-quality stallion and riding horse: Arogno (foaled 1976) is by Flaneur out of Arcticonius XX by Apollonius XX. He was top stallion at the stallion performance testing in Adelheidsdorf in 1979 for his owner and breeder I. I. Wenzel of Hückeswagen.

families near Xanten, and the Reichshof stud, all of which were founded on excellent breeding stock.

In 1979 there were 780 Trakehner mares and fifty-three stallions in Rhineland.

Rhineland-Pfalz/Saarland breeding zone

The federal states of Rhineland-Pfalz and Saarland count as one Trakehner breeding zone. Trakehners are bred in this area in their own right as well as for the purpose of upgrading the local warmblood riding horse to meet modern requirements. Trakehner breeding here has been successfully influenced by the Birkhausen Trakehner stud near Zweibrücken, which was leased to the Trakehner *Verband* in 1960 by the Rhineland-Pfalz authorities. Under the management of the *Verband*, a stud of such high quality developed that it was used to shape Trakehner breeding throughout southwestern Germany. At this stud are about twenty mares almost exclusively descended in a direct line from the female families of the Trakehnen central stud. There are also two select stallions. In particular the lines of Tapete by Pythagoras, Halensee by Hannibal, and Blitzrot by Hirtensang have left their mark at this stud. Apart from cultivating these old and highly esteemed lines, a main priority of the stud is to produce stallions whose breeding and quality will give new momentum to Trakehner breeding and enable it to progress. Stallions such as Carajan, Donauwind, Prince Rouge XX and more recently the large-framed, important Matador have greatly influenced both breeding and competition horse production. Annexed to the stud is a training and marketing centre in which the novice horses are brought on and presented to potential buyers.

Donauwind, the most important stallion from the modern Pregel line, had outstanding breeding qualities. He stood in both Denmark and the USA as well as West Germany, siring licensed stallions and numerous registered broodmares, and transmitting to his progeny first class riding qualities suitable for all branches of equestrian sport. His stallion son Abdullah won an Olympic gold medal for the USA at the Los Angeles Olympics, and has many other international showjumping successes to his name

A broodmare of the very highest calibre is the chestnut Tracht (foaled 1969) by Prince Rouge XX out of Traviata by Impuls, owned and bred by the Birkausen Trakehner stud. She combined the clean limbs and 'finely chiselled' look of the Thoroughbred with the substance, type and outstanding paces of her old, consolidated Trakehner bloodlines.

Since the beginning of the 1960s, the Grumbach stud in the Saarland area has been particularly dominant, achieving great success in both breeding and equestrianism. This stud cultivates the female lines of Feodora and Maskotte (both originating from the Mack-Altof stud), and was responsible for producing the international show jumper Feuervogel.

The Karthäuserhof stud (Werner Tyrell) at Trier-Eitelsbach became the base for the large-framed, substantial chestnut stallion Unesco by Kassius, following the retirement, after long years of useful service, of the highly esteemed Persaldo by Hessenstein.

At the Hof Venusberg stud at Gielert, the stallion Halali by Gabriel was used with an extraordinary measure of success. Halali produced many horses which have been successful in top-level competition. Other Trakehner studs worth mentioning include H. A. Zorn's stud at Nastätten, Lorenz Summa at Saarwellingen, Herbert Jaeckel at Gut Schönberg/Oberwesel, Heinz Leffer at Blieskastel, Willy Schneider at Laubach and Peter Baum at Asbach.

In 1979 there were a total of twenty-eight stallions standing at stud in this breeding zone, nine of which belonged to the Zweibrücken state stud. There were also 394 mares registered with the Trakehner *Verband* in Rheinland Pfalz and Saarland.

Hessen breeding zone

During the 1970s the quality of Trakehner breeding stock produced in the Hessen area rose appreciably. This improvement is due to the fact that several top modern stallions stood in this area at that time. One of the earliest Trakehner studs to be founded was the Biebertal stud at Giessen. This stud, mainly producing greys, was particularly strongly influenced by the blood of the original Trakehner mare Kassette by Harun al Raschid OX. Several large-framed horses with particularly dynamic paces descended from this mare have been produced by the Biebertal stud.

The Im Niedern stud, Gedern, was the base at the start of his career for the stallion Grandezzo by Cher XX, the reserve champion of the 1977 stallion licensing and the performance champion of his year group. This stallion has covered large numbers of mares and has been shown to have uniform and far above average prepotency.

The largest breeding establishment in this zone in recent years has been the Wälderhausen stud at Homberg/Ohm, which has about thirty broodmares. It was the home of the top stallion Ibikus by Hertilas before he was exported to Denmark. Ibikus has been extremely successful as a sire of competition horses as well as breeding stock in both Denmark and West Germany. The Wälderhäusen stud represents some of the best and most highly rated Trakehner bloodlines, and during the 1970s there was a steady rise in the quality of the breeding stock. Other notable modern studs in this area include the Domäne Mechthildhausen at Wiesbaden-Erbenheim; the Hof Altenburg stud at Bad Orb; and Rossbacher Hof at Erbach-

Top stallion of his year group and a typical example of a modern Trakehner was the bay Tannenberg (foaled 1966) by Sterndeuter out of Tanjana by Abendstern. He was bred by Veronika von Schöning at Neversfelde. After standing at stud in West Germany he was exported to America and became one of the most well-known and popular stallions during the early years of the American Trakehner Association, which was formed in the 1970s and is recognised by the Trakehner *Verband* as the official registry for Trakehner horses in North America.

Rossbach, where Condus by Ramzes had a positive effect on Trakehner breeding, especially *vis-à-vis* 'rideability' (easiness to ride). The Rainmühle stud at Griedel and the Wiesengrund stud at Seligenstadt also deserve to be mentioned.

In 1979 the number of registered breeding stock stood at 486 broodmares and thirty-five stallions. Of the stallions, thirteen belonged to the Dillenburg state stud, while the remaining twenty-two stood privately.

Baden-Württemberg breeding zone

Trakehner breeding in the state of Baden-Württemberg is closely linked with the transformation of the Württemberger Warmblood from a farm horse to a competition horse. The Marbach (Baden-Württemberg) central state stud, which also serves as the regional stud for its own immediate area, has played an important role in Trakehner breeding as well as Württemberger breeding. It has a herd of about twenty broodmares of pure Trakehner origin which can be classed as one of the best

One of the best quality stallions to come forward for licensing in recent years was Rantzau's bay stallion Schiwago (1974) by Tannenberg out of Schlobitten by Malachit (Schwalbe – by Totilas – female line). His dam was subsequently exported to Britain where she became the dam of the young stallion Holme Grove Solomon.

A prime example of a Trakehner is the black stallion Schwalbenfreund (1973), by Impuls out of Schwarze Schwalbe by Traumgeist XX bred by the Webelsgrund stud and owned by the Hörstein stud at Alzenau. He was top stallion of the 1975 licensing, and from the point of view of conformation and prepotency he has been one of the most important stallions in modern-day Trakehner breeding.

in West Germany for uniformity and overall quality, and for the clearly defined lines of its mares. Furthermore, the numerous purebred Trakehner 'regional' stallions (for use on mares belonging to the surrounding population) not only fulfilled their purpose in the Württemberger Warmblood transformation programme but have also had a beneficial effect on pure Trakehner breeding in Baden-Württemberg. In 1979 there was a total of twenty-seven purebred Trakehner stallions in the possession of the state stud. In addition to these there were twenty-four purebred Trakehners standing at private studs. This grand total of fifty-one stallions makes Baden-

Württemberg the state with the highest number of Trakehner stallions at stud. In 1979 there were also 478 registered mares in the district.

In recent years breeding stock which have won top prizes and become highly acclaimed for their good breeding points have drawn attention to the southern German studs. One of these which is of particular interest is the Argenhof Trakehner stud at Wangen, where the Zauberfee female line has been cultivated with great success, and where a first-class selection of stallions have stood at stud, including the highly rated sires Prince Condé, Arthus and Marius. Mention should also be made of the Hammetweil stud at Neckartenzlingen, and Pleikarts Försterhof at Heidelberg, where the long-lived stallion Fantast and his progeny produced several outstanding performance horses. The following studs should also be noted: Anton Steidle at Radofzell, the Stall Maro in Freiburg, Läple in Weinsberg and Bayha at Hofgut Kaltenherberge; the Domäne Neuhaus at Bad Mergentheim, Hofgut Schmelze at Rottweil-Zimmern, and Waggershauser at Friedrichshafen.

Bavarian breeding zone

While in the other breeding zones there is a fairly high concentration of Trakehner studs, or there are nuclei of studs within the various areas, in Bavaria the breeders and breeding establishments are mostly very widely spaced. Some of the older and larger studs have become cornerstones of the Bavarian Trakehner breeding industry and centres of activity.

In 1979 there were 349 registered broodmares and twenty-four stallions in Bavaria. Two of these stallions belonged to the Landshut regional state stud.

The Hörstein stud occupies a special place among the private breeding establishments in that for years it stood above-average numbers of outstanding quality stallions, attracting large numbers of mares from all the West German breeding zones as well as from abroad. The stallions Herbststurm and Schwarm stood there for many years before going to Denmark, and the following Hörstein stallions have also been particularly popular because of their good breeding records and riding qualities: Insterruf (foaled in 1972), black, by Schwalbenflug; Istanbul (1972), bay, by Flaneur [exported to Britain in 1987]; Schwalbenfreund (1973), black, by Impuls; Amadeus (1975), dark bay, by Kassiber; Elfenglanz (1971), liver chestnut, by Magnet; and the son of Elfenglanz, Dynamit. The last two stallions named were made available to the German Olympic committee for use in top-level dressage.

Over the years, the pillar of Bavarian Trakehner breeding has been the Nannhofen stud, belonging to the Baroness von Lotzbeck, near Fürstenfeldbruck. For many years this stud stood one of the few available offspring of Abglanz, the chestnut stallion Kassio. Kassio was a top sire who has had a positive effect on Bavarian horse breeding as well as on Trakehner breeding. In the mare herd the lines cultivated in particular include those of Wachau by Semper Idem, and the Gitarre and Kokette families. The Gitarre line produced the famous national champion mare Griseldis by Pindar XX. This mare was bred at Nannhofen (see illustration on p. 48).

For ten years the legendary grey stallion Maharadscha by Famulus stood at the Schwaighof agricultural research station near Nordendorf. This stallion, especially through his son Flaneur, founded one of the most important sire lines in modern Trakehner breeding. Flaneur was born at Schwaighof, which also possesses a broodmare herd of uniform high quality descended mainly from the Cornelia line and the K-line, which traces to the full sisters Kordel and Koralle IV by Jubel, bred at the Prokelwitz stud, Mohrungen, in the 1920s.

The Gut Postschwaige stud has had extraordinary success with home-bred horses. It has produced successful breeding stock, and above all it has distinguished itself in competition, especially eventing. Also among those of particular interest are the following Trakehner breeding establishments: Schralling at Burgkirchen; Gössenreuth at Himmelskron; Miesbach at Stadelberg; and the Pohl family at Ottelsburg.

Trakehner breeding today and its influence on other breeds

If the figures for registered breeding stock in the different zones are added together, the resulting total does credit to the many years of work which went into the reconstruction of Trakehner breeding.

In 1980 there were 4500 live mares registered in the broodmare section of the Trakehner *Verband*'s stud book, and about 300 licensed Trakehner stallions standing at stud. There were 3600 members of the society. It is interesting to note that the number of mares alone doubled in the 1970s, and the Trakehner *Verband* is now numerically one of the largest riding horse breed societies in West Germany. The upward trend was also evident in the years from 1960 to 1970, at a time when German cold- and warmblood breeding in general was having to cut back because the horses being produced were no longer what was wanted.

The market demand for an elegant, versatile, highly bred competition horse was particularly easy to fulfil for the Trakehner breeding industry, because 'riding qualities' had always been a predominant feature of the breeding policy. This explains why all the German warmblood breeds have had recourse to infusions of Trakehner blood at some time or another, and to a greater or lesser extent, as a means of producing as quickly and reliably as possible the desired stamp of riding horse with the necessary performance qualities. Elegance, breeding, presence, and smooth 'light-footed' paces are riding horse characteristics possessed by the Trakehner. In the transformation from farm horse to competition horse which has been successfully carried out with all the German breeds over the last few decades, it is accepted that the Trakehner played a major role in transmitting these 'upgrading' characteristics.

Hanoverian breeding has been closely linked with Trakehner breeding for about 150 years. Back in the nineteenth century many East Prussian stallions stood in Hanover. In the 1930s, Charm's son Fahnenträger sired some valuable breeding stock there. Since some of the stallions from the Georgenburg regional stud and from the 1944 batch of stallions from Trakehnen were evacuated to Lower Saxony, some of them came to be used by the Celle state stud as an upgrading influence in

For conformation and quality, one of the most important stallions in the recent history of Trakehner breeding is the black Inselkönig (1966) by Kapitän out of Insterlied by Stern XX. He was bred by Freiherr von Schoetter at Ägidienberg and spent his later years at Celle, where he was used mainly on Hanoverian mares.

Hanoverian horse breeding. Of these, Termit's son Abglanz, Dampfross's son Semper Idem, and Helikon's son Lateran founded important, now flourishing, sire lines which have left their mark on Hanoverian breeding and have spread far and wide. Hansakapitän, Altan, Cyklon and Humboldt have also made a valuable contribution, and successful use has been made of the stallions Trautmann by Stern XX and Hessenstein by Komet. The last-named stallion, and the black stallion Inselkönig by Kapitän, stood at the Celle state stud. Other Trakehner stallions in private hands are recognised by the Hanoverian breed society, the *Verband Hannoverischer Warmblutzüchter*, and are also very popular with Hanoverian breeders.

In no German state has the necessary transformation from farm horse to competition horse taken such a trouble-free and rapid course as in Baden-Württemberg. The Trakehner was the only breed used in this process. The first step in the upgrading programme was taken when the then director of the Marbach central and regional

The most successful representative of the Dampfross line was the grey stallion Pregel (foaled in 1958) who stood both privately and at the Marbach state stud. His valuable genetic heritage will benefit riding horse breeding for decades to come.

stud brought the Trakehner stallion Julmond (foaled in 1938 by Julianus) to Baden-Württemberg in 1960. This medium-sized chestnut stallion with enormous presence had such effective and excellent prepotency that a memorial stone was erected to him in Marbach on which he is referred to as the 'regenerator of Baden-Württemberg horse breeding'. He was followed by a number of Trakehner stallions known for their prepotency. These stallions were made available for public use at stallion stations around the region. The best of them stood at Marbach, for use on its own mares. Particularly worthy of mention were Schabernack, Ilmengrund, Kastor, Kufstein, Pregel, and more recently Amor. The most important of these is beyond doubt the grey stallion Pregel (1958, by Tropenwald out of Peraea by Hirtensang). He is rightfully described as one of the most prominent and best riding horse sires since the war in the whole of German riding horse breeding.

Many of the stallions which are available to riding horse breeders in Baden-Württemberg have Trakehner sires and are the products of the local warmblood breeding programme. Many others have frequent infusions of Trakehner blood on the female side of their ancestry. In addition to these, in 1980 there were twenty-four purebred Trakehner stallions standing privately which were approved for use as sires in the horse-breeding industry of the region. In the same year, the Marbach state stud also had twenty-five Trakehner stallions which were available for the use of private breeders. Of these Kornett II, Tassilo, Astor, Perfekt and Kufstein in particular have begun to build themselves reputations as sires of performance horses.

The Hessen state stud at Dillenburg usually has a total stallion population of around sixty, of which a relatively large proportion are Trakehners. Thus we see that horse breeding in this region, which is based on Oldenburg foundations, is at present clearly and positively influenced by the strong use of Trakehner stallions. In particular the stallions Kosmos (foaled in 1956), black, by Hansakapitän; Thor (1959), brown, by Humboldt; Helianthus (1961), chestnut, by Altan; Harfner (1961), chestnut, by Poet XX, and Mandant (1964), chestnut, by Thor have stamped both the Trakehner and the Hessen horse.

The Rheinland-Pfalz and the Saarland Warmblood are now one and the same, and controlled by a single breed society. As in Baden-Württemberg and Hessen, the Trakehner has played, and continues to do so, a major and important role in the upgrading, improving and modernising of the warmblood horse in this region. In the 1970s the number of Trakehner stallions available at the Zweibrücken state stud for the use of private breeders was reduced, although in 1979 there were still nine purebred Trakehners out of a total of twenty-four stallions at this time-honoured establishment. Among others, the stallions Schöner Abend, Hortus, Rossini, Marlo, Elfenprinz and Isenstein have been widely used and have had particular influence. The Birkhausen stud near Zweibrücken has played an especially important part in horse breeding in this region.

During the 1970s the Warendorf state stud had the Gunnar stallion Bernstein and the black stallion Garamond by Gabriel standing at Rhineland stallion stations in the capacity of Westphalians. In the 1950s, the Absinth stallion Abschaum was widely used, and the offspring he produced in Westphalia include the DLG stallion Aar, who was the sire of talented competition horses as well as quality breeding stock. [A DLG stallion is one that has represented its breed at a German agricultural society show.] There are Hanoverian stallions at Warendorf which carry the blood of Abglanz, Semper Idem and Lateran, thus perpetuating the Trakehner influence.

It is essentially the Trakehner which has shaped the recently developed Rhineland Warmblood breeding industry. In particular the stallions Hartung, Patron, Abendregen, Bernstein, Borusse, Garamond, Insterfeuer and Frohsinn have been instrumental in giving uniformity and an identity to an up-and-coming breed whose female foundation stock came from a wide range of different backgrounds. Borusse, Patron and Hartung produced successful competition horses with a special talent for jumping. Garamond and Bernstein produced large numbers of mares which won national premiums, plus licensed stallions, from privately owned mares. Most of the stallions standing at stud in this area are in private hands, and Trakehner breeders in particular are playing an important role.

In Oldenburg the transformation of the indigenous heavy coach horse into the desired riding horse has been very successful. The Trakehner stallions Kompass and Herbststurm played their part in this process. The Major stallion Magister stood at stud at the Cappeln stallion station and enjoyed great popularity. Numerous high-class premium mares and Marschall, champion Oldenburg stallion at the DLG show, are among his descendants. More recently the approved Trakehner stallions Harnisch, Kant and Korund have been used as an upgrading influence in the area. Oldenburg breeding has also been influenced indirectly by the extensive use of Hanoverian stallions tracing back to Abglanz, Semper Idem and Lateran.

The Bavarian state stud at Landshut began using Trakehner stallions as an upgrading influence in its area at an early stage. In 1962 the top prize-winning stallion, the black Komet, went to stand at the state-run establishment at Achselschwang. He contributed to the Bavarian horse-breeding industry numerous premium mares and licensed stallions. In 1980 the stallions Mahdi and Magnus stood at the Landeshut state stud with above average results. Privately owned stallions of particular interest which have had considerable influence on horse breeding in this region are the grey Maharadscha and the chestnut Kassio by Abglanz. These are now to be considered as top sires in Trakehner breeding as well as in Bavarian Warm-blood breeding.

By the beginning of the 1980s there was a total of forty-five Trakehner stallions standing at state-owned establishments in West Germany. The number of mares covered by these stallions was above average. The same year the number of stallions

Traditionally the Trakehner *Verband* presents a collection of breeding stock, which match in colour, at the DLG show which is held every two years at a different location. One of the best collections since the war was the group of blacks which was shown at Cologne in 1970: with seven horses the society won two championships, six first prizes and two second prizes.

in private hands was 236. The large number of stallions standing privately is due to the fact that there is no state stud in West Germany dedicated exclusively to the Trakehner and able to supply breeders with Trakehner stallions in sufficient quantity, as is the normal function of state studs in West Germany.

The 250-year history of East Prussian horse breeding gives a good example of the invaluable role played by state studs. Before the Second World War, East Prussia, with its central and regional state studs, was recognised as being the largest reservoir of riding horses in the world. It was there that the genetic heritage was developed which survived the trauma of the Second World War and became an important element in West German horse breeding. A study of the pedigrees of sport and competition horses in catalogues and other publications clearly reveals the important role played by the Trakehner in the development of the various warmblood breeds.

The upgrading and improvement of the German regional breeds with the aim of producing a well-bred, elegant and marketable riding horse is achieved also by the use of English Thoroughbred and to a lesser extent Arab blood. The Trakehner can be considered as a sort of 'bridge' between these two breeds and the warmblood. The pedigree of the Trakehner contains both Thoroughbred and Arab blood, though mainly the former.

English Thoroughbred blood is used in Trakehner breeding at selected larger studs. The Thoroughbred stallions Stern XX, Maigraf XX and Swazi XX were used at the Hunnesrück stud (Lower Saxony), as were Pindar XX at the Schmoel (Panker) stud (Holstein) and the Nannhofen stud (Bavaria); Traumgeist XX and Kreuzritter XX at Rantzau (Holstein); Prince Rouge XX at the Trakehner *Verband*'s Birkhausen stud (Rheinland-Pfalz) and Pasteur XX at the Vogelsangshof stud (Rhineland). These stallions were chosen with particular emphasis on their riding qualities and temperaments. Their achievements on the racetrack were not a primary consideration. Some very high-class stallions have been produced in recent years as the result of these crosses, among them Grandezzo by Cher XX, Mahagoni by Pasteur XX, and Arogno by Flaneur out of a Thoroughbred mare. This has given rise to the claim that the Trakehner breed 'knicks' with the Thoroughbred better than any other German riding horse breed.

So as not to let the Arab influence die out completely, the Trakehner breeding authorities have made a point of promoting some stallions with Arab blood. Among these were Burnus X and Gazal X, and the purebred Arabians Marsuk OX and Karmin OX. Stallions such as Donauwind, Flaneur and Habicht owe their popularity today as sires to the traces of Arab blood in their ancestry.

A collection of bay breeding stock of outstanding quality was shown at the DLG show in 1974 in Frankfurt. The horses showed true breed type and excellent paces – qualities which the Trakehners are successfully transmitting to other warmblood breeds.

Whether the use of English Thoroughbred and Arab blood can have a uniform upgrading effect in warmblood breeding over the course of generations remains to be seen. It must surely be safer to use the Trakehner, which is more likely to pass on the right qualities since its ancestors have been tested for 'rideability' and performance capability and proven themselves suitable as competition horses. The reason for this can be found in the breed's history: the aim of Trakehner breeding, as has been seen, has been mainly to produce horses for the army, and later for sport and competition.

Modern trends in Trakehner breeding

In Trakehner breeding, with the exception of Thoroughbred and Arab, the introduction of outside blood is not allowed. The size – both the height and the size of the frame – has been increased in recent times but without recourse to warmblood stallions of other breeds. The modern Trakehner, as seen at competitions, shows and

The Maharadscha stallion Flaneur (foaled in 1965), an important representative of the male line of Fetysz OX, stands out as a sire of harmonious horses with 'type' and good riding qualities.

auctions, is of a large-framed, versatile, elegant type with an excellent temperament, as required by modern buyers. There are about 300 stallions at stud, and there are three sires in particular which stand out as having had the greatest influence on the breed: they are Impuls, Pregel and Maharadscha, the last-named through his son Flaneur in particular.

The bay stallion Impuls (Jagdheld line), foaled in 1953, by Humboldt out of Italia 54 by Eichendorf, has sixteen licensed stallions and about 100 mares registered with the Trakehner *Verband* among his progeny.

One of the great sires of the postwar period was Impuls (foaled 1953) by Humboldt. He founded a flourishing sire line and produced over 100 registered broodmares and numerous successful competition horses.

The grey stallion Pregel (Dampfross line), foaled in 1958, by Tropenwald out of Peraea 832, is rightly known as the best riding horse sire of the postwar period, and has eleven licensed sons. Of these, Donauwind alone (p. 55), who is the most important, had fourteen licensed sons and over sixty registered daughters in 1979. Donauwind also stood in Denmark for a number of years before finishing his days at stud in the USA.

Maharadscha (Fetysz OX line), foaled in 1957, by Famulus out of Marke 760, was also grey. He has sired eleven stallions, among them Flaneur, who is one of today's

Since 1965 the Trakehner *Verband* has held annual broodmare auctions. The photograph shows the black mare Corona (foaled 1976), by Kassiber out of Coretta by Auftakt, being shown loose before the sale in the 'Holstenhalle', Neumünster. She was bred by H. W. Paul at Rethwisch, and a few months later she successfully represented the Trakehner breed at the first German Riding Horse championships (*Bundeschampionat des Deutschen Reitpferdes*) in Münster-Handorf in 1979.

Opposite page, top
Three-year-old stallions in training at the state stallion testing centre, Adelheidsdorf (Lower Saxony). Here, young stallions at the beginning of their stud career undergo a hundred-day test which is primarily a test of their natural performance qualities and their 'rideability'.

Opposite page, bottom
At the elite Trakehner stallion show in Neumünster in 1974, the two stallions Virgil (right) and Insterruf emerged as champion and reserve champion. Both have since come to occupy prominent positions as sires, and Insterruf has now been imported to the USA.

top stallions. There are also thirteen first-class stallions by Flaneur standing at stud, some of which have themselves had very successful competition careers. All are producing top-quality competition horses themselves, most of which are part-Thoroughbred. As a result of bringing Trakehner breeding in line with market demands through the use of these and other stallions, and thanks also to skilful marketing by the breed authorities, notable successes have been achieved in recent years at auctions and in sport. Mention must be made at this point of the annual Trakehner stallion licensing show, which takes place in October at Neumünster (Holstein). At this event all potential stallions aged two and a half years are subjected to a rigorous examination. In order to earn the coveted licence, they must possess the qualities which will enable them to advance and improve the breed. The stallion auctions are held in Neumünster in conjunction with the licensing. Licensed stallions are sold as potential sires, while the unlicensed ones are sold as particularly well-educated young riding horses. These occasions have become important events in the equestrian calendar. They enjoy international acclaim and attract buyers and spectators from all over the world to the 'Holstenhalle' in Neumünster.

Following the licensing, the young stallions have to undergo performance testing – the so-called 'hundred-day test' – along with potential stallions of other breeds at a special stallion testing centre. At the Adelheidsdorf centre (near Celle) and at Klosterhof Medingen (Lower Saxony) and Marbach (Baden-Württemberg), Trakehners are often the highest placed in the testing.

The Neumünster autumn sale also includes a broodmare auction for selected mares which are guaranteed to be in foal. This is a good opportunity for up-and-coming breeders to acquire suitable breeding material under the guidance of the Trakehner *Verband*. Known, established breeders from Germany and abroad use this occasion to make up any deficiencies in their breeding material.

An important event in the history of Trakehner breeding was the first national Trakehner breeding stock show, the *Bundesschau für Trakehner Zuchtpferde*, which was held at Verden-an-der-Aller in 1975. The best 100 broodmares were examined by a committee of judges and awarded premiums. At this show it became apparent that the Trakehner breed 'type' and the distinctive characteristics of its appearance had survived the thirty-year 'reconstruction'. The elastic, 'light-footed' action of the Trakehners and the overall high quality of the breeding material met with the unanimous approval of all the experts present.

The largest Trakehner breed show in the 1970s was the *Jubiläumsschau für Trakehner Hengste*, which was held on 21 October 1977 at Neumünster. The four-hour programme, during which the best stallions and the most successful top-level competition horses were displayed, marked to the day the thirtieth anniversary of the setting up of the Trakehner *Verband* in West Germany. Experts from all over the world were enthusiastic about the well-presented programme and were given a demonstration of the many outlets for this versatile breed in sport and in the leisure field.

One handicap suffered by Trakehner breeding is the fact that there are still too few Trakehners on the competition scene. One reason for this is that only relatively few Trakehner breeders are active riders, so that Trakehner breeding lacks the wide network of committed riders which other breeds have. The other reason is that highly talented dressage, jumping and eventing horses are often bought by people who only ride as a hobby. Efforts being made in the private sector to find 'undiscovered talent' and to place horses with 'top potential' in the right hands can help in this respect. One example of such a scheme is the Trakehner Riding Horse auction held every spring at the Darmstadt Riding Club's centre in Kranichstein. The young riding horses are given several weeks training and assessment under saddle and then sold as suitable either for competition or for leisure riding. This is one way of making it possible for more Trakehners to lead successful competition careers.

4 Trakehner competition horses in the twentieth century

Particularly in the period between the two world wars, East Prussian horses were very famous for their toughness and endurance as performance horses for use in many different fields of activity. Their extraordinary success in the Olympic Games, in the famous steeplechases of the period such as the 'von-der-Goltz-Querfeldein-rennen' and the 'Pardubice', and in national and international competitions in all branches of equestrian sport, earned the breed worldwide renown.

The success of East Prussian horses in the Olympic Games dates back to the 1912 Copenhagen Olympics. They were then mostly owned by foreign riders, as were those seven which took part in the Paris Olympics in 1924. Of these the Trakehner Piccolomini, ridden by General Linder, won the dressage gold medal for Sweden. The gelding Balte, a member of the Dutch team and bred at Dr Rothe's Tollmingkehmen stud (which also produced subsequent Olympic medal winners Kronos and Absinth), won the three-day event gold medal under the name King of Heart. Ten East Prussian horses took part in the 1928 Olympics in Amsterdam. They were highly placed in both the dressage and the three-day event.

The most noteworthy performance by East Prussian horses was at the 1936 Berlin Olympics in the three-day event and the dressage. The two blacks, Kronos and Absinth, both by Carol and bred by C. Rothe at Samonienen, won the gold and silver medals for dressage in the individual section, ridden by H. Pollay and F. Gerhard. Together with Rittmeister von Oppeln-Bronikowski on the seventeen-year-old East Prussian Gimpel (a chestnut gelding by Wandersmann XX, bred at the Totenhöfer stud, Birkenfeld), they also won the gold medal in the team event. Gimpel's achievement was particularly creditable in view of his age and the fact that he had also taken part in the 1928 Amsterdam Olympics. The three-day event was won by Ludwig Stubbendorff on the East Prussian Nurmi by Merkur, bred by H. Paul at Rudwangen. (Herr Paul's son is now breeding Trakehners at Rethwisch, near Preetz, in Schleswig-Holstein.) Together with the chestnut East Prussian gelding Fasan (by Burckhardt XX, bred by Siegfried at Skandlack and ridden by Rittmeister Lippert) and the Thoroughbred Kurfürst ridden by Freiherr von Wangenheim, Germany also won the team gold medal in this event.

East Prussia has also produced some excellent show jumpers. When the German

(*Above*) The 1936 Berlin Olympics were one of the most successful for horses of East Prussian origin. The individual silver medal and the team gold medal for dressage were won by the black Absinth (foaled 1926) by Carol out of Estrella by Amur, bred by Carl Rothe at Samonienen and ridden by Major Friedrich Gerhard. Absinth was a three-quarter brother to Kronos, who was bred at the same stud. (*Left*) Nurmi (foaled 1925) by Merkur out of Najade by Amtmann, ridden by Hauptmann Ludwig Stubbendorff, was a prime example of the toughness and readiness to perform of East Prussian horses, and was also the perfect example of a horse in balance. He was the three-day-event individual and team champion at the 1936 Berlin Olympics. Bred by Hans Paul, Rudwangen.

team won the Prix des Nations in New York in 1935, the best individual performance was by the grey East Prussian Dedo by Deo Fido, bred by Kullat at Gr. Kackschen. Other East Prussians who rose to fame as show jumpers were Kampfgesell, Morgenglanz, Der Mohr, Üblick, Tasso, Schorsch and Kampfer, to mention just a few.

The East Prussians are particularly well represented in the lists of winners of the famous Pardubice (Czechoslovakia), which is still considered to be the toughest of the continental steeplechases. It is run on a cross-country course of about 7 kilometres (4½ miles) which includes about thirty difficult fences. Between 1921, when racing resumed after the First World War, and the outbreak of the Second World War, this race was won by the following East Prussian horses:

1923 Landgraf II by Irrwisch II, bred by Dr von Siegfried, Karben
1924 Herero by Shilfa XX, bred at Trakehnen central stud
1925 Landgraf II by Irrwisch II
1928 Vogler by Christian de Wet XX, bred at Trakehnen central stud
1929 Ben Hur by Benjamin XX, bred by Gruber, Lenkutschen
1932 Remus by Wolkenflug (born in Graditz but of pure Trakehner origin)
1933 Remus by Wolkenflug
1935 Herold by Cornelius, bred by Lengnik, Neu-Lappönen
1936 Herold by Cornelius

Soon after the Second World War, when performance sports were resumed, Trakehner dressage, event and show-jumping horses again played a major role and came to the attention of the riding public through their numerous successes. Among those who achieved consistently high levels of success were the black Fanal by Hausfreund (Trakehnen central stud), and the bay mare Thyra by Trebonius XX.

Opposite page, top
The black Kronos (foaled 1928) by Carol out of Eule by Larifari, bred by Carl Rothe, Samonienen, and ridden by Oberleutnant Heinz Pollay, won the individual and team gold medals for dressage.

Opposite page, bottom
The chestnut gelding Gimpel (foaled 1919), by Wandersmann XX out of Zigeunerin by Adler, bred at the Totenhofer stud, Birkenfeld, showed extraordinary stamina and readiness to perform, continuing until quite advanced in years. He was placed sixth in dressage at the 1928 Amsterdam Olympics and, ridden by Rittmeister von Oppeln-Bronikowski, he won the team gold medal for dressage, with Kronos and Absinth, at the 1936 Berlin Olympics at the age of seventeen.

The grey Herold (foaled 1925), by Cornelius out of Aula by Alpenjäger, bred by Lengnik at Neu-Lappönen, was twice the winner of the great Pardubice race, the toughest of the continental steeplechases. Five other East Prussians are among the winners of this tough performance test.

Opposite page, top
A dressage horse of great character was the original Trakehner-bred black horse Fanal by Hausfreund, who was still winning advanced dressage competitions in 1956 at the age of twenty with the renowned German dressage rider Otto Lörke. He also became the 'schoolmaster' of Olympic riders Liselott Linsenhoff and Ida Freiin von Nagel.

Opposite page, bottom
The first outstanding Trakehner dressage horse of the postwar period was Thyra by Trebonius XX out of Panela by Carneval. Ridden by Rosemarie Springer (pictured) and Willi Schultheiss in the 1950s and 1960s, she was placed over 150 times in advanced dressage classes. In 1955, 1956 and 1959 she was the winner of the German Dressage Derby.

The bay Tantalus by Impuls out of Tanagra by Bussard (bred by Fritz Bähre at the Webelsgrund stud) was one of Rosemarie Springer's best-known competition horses at the beginning of the 1960s. She rode him to victory in numerous riding horse championships and riding horse performance competitions.

Ridden by the past master of German dressage riding, Otto Lörke, Fanal recorded in his career seventy-one wins in dressage competitions, of which twenty-nine were at medium and twenty-eight at advanced level. He was a truly exceptional horse. Even when he was over twenty years old he was still competing with great success in advanced dressage – not only winning, but leaving the rest of the field standing! Thyra was ridden by both Rosemarie Springer and Willi Schultheiss. Among her successes were three wins in the German Dressage Derby in Hamburg in 1955, 1956 and 1959. Altogether she achieved sixty-three wins and was placed 163 times in her career.

The first purebred Trakehner to represent Germany in the Olympic Games after the end of the Second World War was Perkunos, whose sire was the regional state stallion Lustig by Tempelhüter. Perkunos was bred by Freiherr von der Leyen at Hasselpusch in the Heiligenberg district. He arrived in West Germany in 1945 as a very ordinary two-year-old, having survived the trek from East Prussia with his breeder. In 1948 he went to the stables of the dressage rider Hannelore Weygand in Düsseldorf. In 1956 she competed on him in the Stockholm Olympics, where she was placed ninth in the dressage in the individual section, and was a member of the team which won the silver medal. The other members of the team were Liselott Linsenhoff on Adular by Oxyd (Trakehner) and Anneliese Schaurte-Küppers on Afrika who was also by Oxyd. In his career, Perkunos won fifty dressage competitions and was placed in 160. He lived to the age of twenty-two.

The second Olympic dressage horse of Trakehner extraction is the black Ultimo, a consistent performer with his rider Gabriella Grillo, and winner of many important competitions. It was she who was responsible for turning him into a top-class dressage horse. His greatest achievement was winning the team gold medal at the Bromont (Canada) Olympics in 1976. He was fourth in the individual placings. The breeder of this successful horse was A. Nörenberg of Rothensande. He was reared by Krossa at the Gutsverwaltung Siek. The partnership of Gabriella Grillo and Ultimo had a long catalogue of successes to its credit: in 1977 they won the German Championships and the German Dressage Derby in Hamburg-Flottbek, in 1977 and 1979 they were members of the team which won the gold medal in the European Championships, in 1978 they were members of the gold medal winning team at the World Championships held in Goodwood, England, and were placed fourth as individuals. In 1980, Ultimo was again the winner of the German Dressage Derby and the German Championships. With these and many other successes behind him, he has come to epitomise the ideal Trakehner competition horse.

A highly talented show jumper was the grey Spritzer by Famulus out of Meta by Absalon. Ridden by Karl-Heinz Giebmanns, this horse was one of Germany's top jumpers in the mid-1960s.

Opposite page
The mare Illusion (foaled 1963) by Flugsand out of Inka by Humboldt, was the winner of numerous medium and advanced level dressage competitions for Harry Boldt. She was bred by Ernst Schlegel, Detmold.

The chestnut stallion Azurit (foaled 1973) by My Lunaria XX out of Arietta by Coriolan was competed with some success by Swiss dressage world champion Christine Stückelberger. Bred by Franz Lage, Neuwetterade.

Opposite page
The black stallion Habicht (foaled 1967) by Burnus out of Hallo by Goldregen, owned by the Association for Furthering and Maintaining the Warmblood Breed of Trakehner Origin, was made available to the German Olympic Committee for its three-day-event stable in Warendorf in 1975. Among his successes with his rider Martin Plewa were the best performance by a German team member in the international three-day event at Burghley, 1976, and winner of the international three-day event at Achselschwang, 1977. He was bred by the Stut stud at Volksdorf, and raised at the Kurhessisch Foundation, Schmoel.

Ultimo (Gabriela Grillo), Fabian (Dr Reiner Klimke), and Kleopatra (Georg Theodorescu) in 'passage' during a *pas de trois* at the Bremen Hallenturniers 1980.

Opposite page
A horse who showed an extraordinary talent for dressage from an early age was the grey stallion Fabian by Donauwind out of Fawiza by Maharadscha. Seen here as an eight-year-old with his rider, Dr Reiner Klimke, this licensed stallion won an advanced-level dressage competition at his first attempt. Bred by the Birkhausen Trakehner stud.

In step and in perfect harmony: *pas de deux* by the black mares Istria (foaled 1965), by Obermaat XX out of Isis by Impuls (on left), and Kleopatra (foaled in 1968), by Halali out of Kore by Boris. Ridden by Inge and Georg Theodorescu.

Opposite page
Ultimo, ridden by Gabriela Grillo, at the 1976 Montreal Olympics, where he was fourth in the individual placings and a member of the gold-medal winning team. His other great successes include world champion (team) 1978, German champion 1979, European (team) champion 1979, German Dressage Derby winner 1977 and 1980. Bred by A. Nörenberg, Rotensande. He competed with success well into the 1980s.

Another top-class Trakehner dressage horse was Hirtentraum, ridden by Uwe Sauer. A son of Traumgeist XX and bred by the Schmoel (Panker) stud in Holstein, by 1980 Hirtentraum had the following successes to his credit: German Championships – Reserve Champion 1978; European Championships – 5th place 1977, 7th place 1979; World Championships – 9th place 1978; Gold Medal (team) at Goodwood (England) 1980. This horse is an example of the legendary tenacity and readiness to perform of the Trakehner, in that his form and consistency in top-level national and international advanced dressage competitions steadily improved over the years (see illustration on p. 108).

Trakehners have also distinguished themselves in show-jumping competitions in the period since the end of the Second World War. At the beginning of the 1960s the outstanding grey Spritzer by Famulus, bred by Peter Mott at Keppeln, was one of Germany's top show jumpers. With his rider K. H. Giebmanns he was a member of winning German Prix des Nations teams. In the 1970s, four horses in particular stood out for their achievements and the high levels of prize money they won in top-level national and international show jumping. They were the chestnut mare Biene by Carajan (Hugo Simon), the chestnut Feuervogel by Prince Rouge XX, the bay Hanko by Kobalt (Wolfgang Knorren) and the grey Hyppi by Himalaja (Elma Gundel).

A top three-day-event horse was the black stallion Habicht by Burnus (Martin Plewa), among whose successes was the international event at Achselschwang in 1977. At the European Championships at Burghley in 1977, the Trakehner Akzent by Helianthus, ridden by Hanna Huppelsberg-Zwöck, helped win the team silver medal for Germany.

Numerous Trakehners also competed very successfully at lower and intermediate levels in all branches of equestrian sport during the 1970s. In the 1979 season, for example, 1500 Trakehner horses won around 470,000 DM in Category A and B competitions [i.e. of regional level and above; horses must be registered with the German Federation]. These figures are rising steadily from year to year.

5 Recent developments

The Trakehner in West Germany in the 1980s

The 1980s saw a continuing increase in the popularity of the Trakehner breed, not only as a pure breed in itself, but as a competition horse and as a source for out-crossing and modernising blood for the other West German warmblood breeds. Because of this, there are now nearly 1400 foals registered every year and a number of the most popular stallions such as Consul (by Ramzes) and Arogno (by Flaneur out of Arcticonius XX by Apollonius XX) cover over forty mares a year in their districts, when standing against other locally based warmblood stallions.

An allied development, which reflects the increasing demand for proven Trakehner bloodlines in competition horses, was the introduction in 1985 of optional

Bartholdy (by Mahagoni out of Balaika by Polifax), the stallion grading champion in 1982 in Neumünster, champion in the ridden test in 1983 and DLG champion in 1986, is already proving equally successful as a sire, with graded sons in the USA and West Germany and champion broodmare daughters. (*Photo: © Werner Ernst*)

four-week-long mare testing at two stations in Handorf and Medingen, in addition to the already established optional one-day field test regularly held at Traventhal. The long-term effects of this mare testing policy cannot yet be fully analysed, but they are already proving popular with mare owners.

With the outstanding success of such horses as Abdullah (by Donauwind), the international market of Trakehners with proven competition bloodlines is also increasing. In 1988, for instance, when sale prices for Trakehner riding horses at auction ranged from top prices of £18,000 to £26,500 ($29,000 to $42,000) for top-class horses and from £6000 to £7000 ($9000 to $11,500) for good all-round animals, one horse sold at the PSI Sales fetched a record Trakehner price of £86,000 ($138,000). In the same period, two-year-old approved stallions sold at Neumünster cost their new owners from £7200 to £16,800 ($11,500 to $27,000), with the reserve champion of the grading and three premium stallions fetching an average of £36,000 ($58,000), and seven of the stallions sold finding new homes abroad.

Among the most important and desired Trakehner bloodlines in West Germany in the 1980s have been those of Mahagoni (by Pasteur XX out of Maharani II by Flaneur) and his son Bartholdy (out of a Polifax mare), Consul, Habicht, and the Flaneur son Arogno. However, because of the increasing international interest in warmblood breeding, a substantial amount of the current influence of such stallions as these – and of other such successful sires as Donauwind and Ibikus – appears in the pedigrees of horses born in Denmark, Great Britain and the USA, and it is in this context that the Trakehner of today should also be considered.

Denmark and Sweden

As is the case with a number of countries outside West Germany, purebred Trakehners foaled in Denmark can receive either locally issued (but Trakehner *Verband* approved) Trakehner papers or the papers of the local warmblood breeding society (in this case Danish Warmblood papers), according to the grading status of the parents, with partbred Trakehners always receiving warmblood papers rather than partbred Trakehner papers. This is because many imported Trakehner stallions and mares are graded into the warmblood breeding studbooks of their new home country in order to provide valuable new bloodlines. It is principally for this reason that Denmark has become the home of a number of famous Trakehner stallions over the past twenty-five years, including such influential stock getters as Donauwind (by Pregel out of Donaulied von Schimmelhof by Boris), Ibikus (by Hertilas out of Isolda by Impuls) and Gunnar (by Komet out of Gudrun by Abendstern). Trakehner sires in Denmark have therefore frequently covered not only Trakehner mares (of whom there are a considerable number) but also a wide variety of warmblood mares of various other breeds. This out-crossing has been a vital factor in the development of the Danish Warmblood, for not only has it produced some notable competition horses, but also a number of influential stallions including Galanthus (by Gunnar out of a Hanoverian mare by Wohler), Dolomit (by Donauwind out of a Danish Warmblood mare by the Hanoverian stallion Solist) and Kawango (by Ibikus out of another Solist mare), who look set to carry the influence of their sires on to another generation. Donauwind also found fame in Denmark as the sire of the outstanding broodmare Diana (out of a Danish Warmblood mare by the Hanoverian Atlantic). Diana was the first-ever gold medal mare in Denmark and has already produced two graded stallion sons, Domino (by the Hanoverian Luxemburg) and the all-conquering Diamond (by the Hanoverian Allegro), who was supreme champion at

Gunnar (by Komet out of Gudrun by Abendstern), as a young stallion at the Panker stud. Gunnar stood at stud in Denmark from 1969 to 1971, siring a number of notable competition horses, and three graded Danish Warmblood stallions, before being reimported into West Germany. (*Photo:* © *Werner Menzendorf*)

his grading and was described by Dr Hanfried Haring as the outstanding model of a modern riding horse sire.

As many of the top bloodlines in Denmark today have their roots in imported Swedish Warmblood bloodlines, upon whose breeding policies the Danish Warmblood is closely modelled, it is perhaps not surprising that Trakehners have provided such a valuable infusion of compatible blood. Swedish breeders have themselves used a significant percentage of old East Prussian blood over the past 100 years, and even in the immediate postwar years, when the future of the Trakehner breed as a whole was in a parlous state, such stallions as Heristal (by Hyperion out of Heta by Paradox XX), Polarstern (by Portwein out of Filiale IV by Alibaba) and Unikum (by Traumgeist XX out of Amadea by Aquavit) found their way to the Swedish State Stud at Flyinge and made a permanent impact on the Swedish breed.

Great Britain

Ever since 1960, when the Muschamp Stud imported the graded stallion Korsar (by Hansakapitän out of J Kordel by Indra) and two mares (Teri and Guntramis), interest in the Trakehner breed has been growing steadily. However, until recently the development of an organised breeding policy was hampered by the existence of two conflicting breeding and registration organisations, the British Trakehner Association and the Trakehner Breeders Society of Great Britain, who both claimed to

Unikum (by Traumgeist XX out of Amadea by Aquavit) stood at the Swedish State Stud at Flyinge from 1964 to 1977.

represent the breed. Fortunately, this difficult situation was finally resolved early in 1989, when – with the encouragement of the Trakehner *Verband* – the registries and membership of both organisations joined together to form the Trakehner Breeders Fraternity of Great Britain (or TBF), which is now the sole official body concerned with Trakehner breeding in Great Britain.

Under the watchful eye of official Trakehner *Verband* judges, the TBF now grades its own stock, brands them with their own adapted version of the Trakehner brand, and issues the necessary registration documents. As yet, however, because of limited numbers and finances the TBF is unable to organise a full 100-day test at a central location, and performance testing takes the form of a one-day event preceded by qualifying competitions. This performance test is compulsory for stallions and optional for mares.

Many British-based Trakehners are also used extensively for warmblood breeding purposes. Most of the Trakehner mares and stallions used at stud in Great Britain are therefore also graded into the appropriate breeding studbooks of the British Warm-Blood Society (the BWBS) and a substantial number of their part-bred Trakehner foals can therefore be registered with, and receive papers from, the BWBS.

Despite the rather confusing organisation of Trakehner breeding in Great Britain, a number of significant Trakehner stallions were imported during the 1980s. These included Holme Grove Stud's Istanbul (by Flaneur out of Idyll by Abendstern) and Mr D. Clarke's Illuster (by Osterglanz XX out of Indiana by Kurfürst). Both of these stallions were already proven producers in West Germany, where Istanbul had already sired a number of noted broodmares and Illuster's daughter Corna had become Riding Horse Champion of all breeds in West Germany in 1985. Both stallions have stood to full books of quality Trakehner and warmblood mares since their arrival, and Holme Grove Stud in particular is the base for some top-quality mares, including StPrSt Schlobitten (by Malachit out of Majanka) who is the dam of the 1976 Neumünster champion Schiwago (by Tannenberg), and StPrSt Marcella (by Postmeister out of a Major mare), herself already the dam of a champion foal in Britain. Since being imported Schlobitten has produced a British-born colt Holme Grove Solomon (by Fernando), who was given temporary covering permission by the TBF in 1988 and by the BWBS in 1989.

Some other outstanding mares have also been imported, including two by the Secretary of the TBF, Mr David Horn. They are the premium mares StPrSt Roma II (by Ferlin out of a mare by Sterndeuter) who was a Verden prizewinner, and Fleuron (by Patron XX and also out of a Sterndeuter mare). The mare grading champion

97

(*Above*) Corna, the Champion Riding Horse of all breeds in West Germany in 1985. This mare is by Illuster, who is now at stud in Great Britain (*Photo:* © *Jean Christen*). (*Opposite page, top*) Illuster (by Osterglanz XX out of Indiana by Kurfürst) imported into Great Britain by Mr D. Clarke in 1985, and equally popular with both Trakehner and warmblood breeders. (*Opposite page, bottom*) Istanbul (by Flaneur out of Idyll by Abendstern), imported into Great Britain in 1986 as the foundation stallion of the Holme Grove Stud.

Mr C. Horn's StPrSt Roma II (by Ferlin out of a Sterndeuter mare), a prizewinner at Verden now producing high-quality foals in Great Britain. (*Photo:* © *Werner Ernst*)

StPrSt Copelia (by Bartholdy out of Cordula by Schiwago) has also recently been imported by Miss Neal and Mr Passetti for breeding purposes.

At present, apart from Solomon's temporary covering permission, only two other Trakehners foaled in Great Britain have been accepted as graded by the TBF, and these are the two sons of the Russian mare Opushka (by Oplot). They are respectively Mrs Yvonne Skinner's Fleetwater Olympus (by Downlands Hasardeur) and Mrs D. Johnson's son of Muschamp Danube, Fleetwater Opposition (who was Junior European Three-Day-Event Champion before retiring to stud). As well as breeding these young stallions, Mrs Louise King's Fleetwater Stud is also the home of the TBF graded stallion Fleetwater Achtermann (by Epos out of Ambosspolka by

Polar) who is leaving some nice foals, mostly to warmblood and Thoroughbred mares.

Fleetwater Olympus' sire, Heath Farm Stud's Downlands Hasardeur (by Schwalbenflug out of Herbstwolke by Erzand), was originally imported by Mrs Marion Hewitt, as was the stallion Downlands Isolan (by Donauwind out of Imortelle by Herzbube) who is now the property of Mrs Rebecca Whitcombe, the present owner of the Downlands prefix. Downlands Isolan has so far concentrated on his competition career as a dressage horse, and as this is also the plan for the new young Downlands stallion, Downlands Zauberstab (by Tenor out of Zauberlicht II by Mahagoni), it will be hard to assess their success as stallions for some years to come.

Downlands Isolan's three-quarter brother, Mrs G. Evans Danish-bred Trakehner Cannabis (by Donauwind out of Catya by Herzbube), is the only other direct representative of the Donauwind male line in Britain, but his career as a show jumper – and the fact that although graded with the BWBS he has not yet attended a TBF grading – means that he has not been used for Trakehner breeding, although he is growing in popularity amongst warmblood mare owners because of his competition record.

In addition to these more recent importations, during the whole of the period since 1960 the Muschamp Stud has continued to breed Trakehners, with Korsar's replacement, the Donauwind half-brother Muschamp Danube (by Isenstein out of Donaulied von Schimmelhof by Boris), proving himself to be a notable sire of both competition horses and broodmares, and the stud's newest addition Muschamp Mauersee (by Arrak out of Marcella by Herzbube) looking set to follow in his footsteps.

Donauwind's half-brother Muschamp Danube (by Isenstein out of Donaulied von Schimmelhof) stood for most of the 1970s and 1980s at Mr Lorch's Muschamp Stud, and was one of the most influential sires in Trakehner breeding in Great Britain during that time.

As yet it is not possible to assess the long-term impact of Trakehner breeding on the British competition horse scene. Both Trakehner and warmblood breeding in Great Britain are still in their early years, with only a very limited number of home-bred sires at stud, and few horses old enough to compete under saddle. However, with the quality of stock so far imported, and a number of studs already building on established foundations, continued growth in the numbers of owners, breeders and foals registered looks to be the future of the Trakehner in Great Britain.

North America

In recent years the Trakehner has been the subject of a spectacular rise in popularity in North America, although by 1989 it was possible to see a considerable reduction in the number of stallions at public stud, possibly because of the rules relating to transported semen imposed by the American Trakehner Association, the official organisation in North America recognised by the Trakehner *Verband*. (A second society, the North American Trakehner Association, also exists, but as it accepts a high percentage of Polish and Russian bloodlines which do not qualify as authentic pure Trakehners in the eyes of the Trakehner *Verband* in West Germany, its studbooks are not officially recognised by the *Verband*.) Interestingly, the annual stallion issue of *The Chronicle of the Horse*, which is probably the best guide to the comparative popularity of the warmblood breeds in North America, carried 81 advertisements for Trakehner stallions in 1984, 138 advertisements in 1985 (a sum equal to nearly 60 per cent of the total Trakehner stallion numbers in West Germany at that time), but only 29 in 1988. Hopefully, this downturn is only temporary, as some outstanding Trakehner stallions have been imported into North America over the years. However, as there is evidence that some competition riders and breeders in the USA have been less than satisfied with the sometimes temperamental attitude of Trakehners to work under saddle, it is possible that the enthusiasm for Trakehners in America is on the wane.

As is the case in many parts of the Trakehner breeding world, the influence of Donauwind is paramount in the USA. Not only did he end his long and successful stud career at Yancey Farms in Texas, where (as he was already the sire of twenty graded stallions and 100 graded broodmares in Europe) he was immediately popular with breeders, but he was also the most sought-after Trakehner sire of the later 1980s. Williamsburg Farm's Abdullah (by Donauwind out of Abiza by Maharad-scha) was imported into America *in utero* and subsequently gained an Olympic Gold

The Olympic Gold Medallist in Los Angeles in 1984, Abdullah (by Donauwind out of Abiza by Maharadscha) is probably the most successful Trakehner of all time in international show jumping. Shown here at the Hamburg Jumping Derby, he is now at stud at Williamsburg Farm in New York State. Abdullah was imported into the USA *in utero*. (*Photo: © Werner Ernst*)

medal in show jumping at Los Angeles in 1984, as well as winning a World Cup final and helping his rider Conrad Holmfield to win the World Championship. Not surprisingly, his semen is in demand all over the world by competition horse breeders.

Donauwind's home at Yancey Farms is also the base for the stallions Falke (by Grimsel out of Fawiza by Maharadscha), who already has a graded son and a champion broodmare graded daughter to his credit in West Germany, and the Mahagoni son Mahon (out of Marussja by Habicht).

Two other proven sires to stand in North America have been Diamond L Trakehner Stud's Insterruf (who, as the sire of four graded stallions, showed his versatility

Morgenglanz (by Abglanz out of Mrakel by Altan), shown at Hunnesrück as a two year old, was top stallion at Trakehner Gestüt Wayne for many years, and a noted sire of both breeding stock and competition horses.

by working as a ranch horse when not occupied with stud duties), and Zeitgeist Trakehner Farms Condus (sire of the Pan American Games dressage silver medallist Chrysos, himself a graded Westphalian stallion imported into the USA).

The Trakehner with probably the longest stud career so far in North America is Trakehner Gestut Wayne's Neumünster champion Morgenglanz (by Abglanz out of Mrakel by Altan), who sired a considerable number of top-class competition horses and the outstanding American-born Trakehner stallion Traum (out of Traumerei by Schabernack). Trakehner Gestut Wayne is also the home of Morgenglanz's grandson Troy (by Ameigo out of Traumfee by Morgenglanz) and Troubadour (by Flaneur out of Trene by Alabaster XX), the Trakehner stallion who was Christine Stückelburger's reserve mount for the 1988 Olympics.

Of the younger stallions at stud in North America, a number achieved top-class grading results at grading in West Germany, including Doomhof Farm's Elgius (by Mackensen out of El Armania by Padparadscha), who was reserve champion at Neumünster in 1982, Wonderland Farm's Donauschimmer (by Valentin out of Donauwinsel von Schimmelhof by Poet XX), who was champion of his performance testing, and Zauberklang (by Prince Condé out of Zauberspiel by Impuls), who was reserve champion in his performance test and is already the sire of proven dressage horses in the USA.

With outstanding sires such as these, and considerable financial backing from interested owners and breeders, it has been possible for Trakehner breeding to make great advances in a very few years. Full 100-day performance tests on Trakehner *Verband* lines are already held, branding with the special ATA brand takes place throughout the continent, and a new full-time secretariat took over all the administration functions of the ATA in mid 1989. This initial success, along with the increasing percentage of wins by Trakehners under saddle in affiliated competitions and in-hand (or 'on the line') at such prestige events as the breeding classes at 'Dressage at Devon', would appear to show that the position of the purebred Trakehner is very healthy in North America at the moment, but the lack of support it is now receiving from a wide range of competition riders may result in problems in the future.

Unfortunately, it is not possible to assess accurately how influential the Trakehner has been or will be in helping to produce a North American warmblood horse, as there is no overall authoritative warmblood breeding organisation on the North American continent. This is chiefly because many new breeders mistakenly tend to breed Hanoverian to Hanoverian, Dutch Warmblood to Dutch Warmblood, Oldenburg to Oldenburg and so on regardless, in a misguided attempt to keep these essentially cross-bred, district-based breeds 'pure' – thus ignoring the essential modernising merits of the Trakehner breeds when they are needed most. Perhaps with the rising awareness of the need to follow good European practice, and the reliance on infusions of Trakehner blood which that brings, Trakehner breeding stock will find its true all-round value appreciated in North America in the coming years.

6 Conclusion

The evolution of the East Prussian Warmblood of Trakehner Origin – nowadays known for short as the Trakehner – is inextricably linked with the turbulent and often tragic history of Germany's eastern territories. The breeders of East Prussia and the now defunct East Prussian breed authorities can be thanked for creating a horse whose performance has earned it worldwide acclaim. The unswerving devotion of the East Prussian people to this horse has enabled it to survive the greatest threat to its existence. This successful regeneration from the small number of animals which remained, in the face of so many difficulties and outside the country of origin, is unique in the history of animal breeding.

Trakehner-based breeding is also carried out on a small scale in the Soviet Union, and traces back to stock which fell into Russian hands in 1945. In Poland, which has more horses than any other European country, the Trakehner breed is referred to as the Wielkopolska, and is bred at several state studs. Denmark, the USA, Switzerland and Great Britain have their own Trakehner breed societies which work in close

The Trakehner brand. (*Left*) from 1787 onwards, all horses born at Trakehnen were branded with a single, seven-pronged elk's antler on the right thigh. (*Centre*) all foals out of mares registered in the stud book are branded with a single elk's antler, with a bow over it, on the left thigh. (*Right*) foals out of main stud book mares are branded with a pair of elk's antlers on the left thigh. All mares registered in the main stud book are branded with a smaller version of the pair of antlers on the left side of the neck.

liaison with the Trakehner *Verband* in Germany, and a number of other countries, including Italy, Colombia and Argentina, have imported Trakehner breeding stock on a lesser scale.

With a score of 4500 registered broodmares and 300 licensed stallions, the Trakehner *Verband* is one of Germany's largest breed societies. The horses bearing the brand of the elk's antlers are known and have distinguished themselves in all branches of equestrianism both in Germany and abroad. This brand is a trademark, and as such enjoys international protection.

Following the years of successful reconstruction since 1945, we can truthfully say that the Trakehner has found a new home.

Opposite page
Hirtentraum (foaled 1967) by Traumgeist XX, ridden by Uwe Sauer. He was the winner of numerous dressage competitions at advanced level, and one of the great dressage horses of modern times. Bred by Kurhessische Hausstiftung, Gutsverwaltung Schmoel; owned by H. S. Struck, Hamburg.

The new generation of the 1980s looks expectantly forward: this chestnut colt foal by Flaneur out of Arcticonius XX by Apollonius is a full brother to the stallions Avignon, Arogno and Acajou, and gives an idea of the quality which can be expected of what is at the same time a very old breed and a very young one.

Bibliography

Heck, Holger and Schietinger, Frank *Die berühmtesten Trakehner Deutschlands*, Friedberg/Hessen, 1986

Heling, Martin. *Trakehnen*, Munich–Bonn–Vienna, 1959

von Henninges, Jürgen. *Stutbuch von Trakehnen*, vol. 6, Brunswick, 1979

Machin Goodall, Daphne. *The flight of the East Prussian horses*, Newton Abbot, 1975

Schilke, Fritz. *Trakehner Pferde einst und jetzt*, Munich, 1974. English translation by Helen K. Gibble, *Trakehner horses then and now*. Norman, Oklahoma, 1977

Trakehner Almanach magazine. An English-language abstract is published annually.

Trakehner Verband. *Trakehner Hengstbuch*, Hamburg, 1975

Trunz, Hansheinrich. *Pferde im Lande des Bernsteins*, Berlin–Hamburg, 1979

von Velsen, Eberhard and Ernst, Werner. *Trakehner heute*, Bad Homburg, 1979

Index of horses' names

Numbers in italics refer to illustrations

118